To Mary

lcc
xx

Made in Newcastle
Visual Culture

Edited by Hilary Fawcett

Very best wishes, Jackie

Best wishes for your 'retirement' Julie

Dear mary
Thanks for all your hard work
all the best for the future
Biddy X

Best wishes
Mandy.

Northumbria University Press

Somehow I think i'll see you again - w/boy guesthouse!!.
Susannah

Very Best Wishes and thanks
Graeme

Published by Northumbria University Press
Trinity Building, Newcastle upon Tyne NE1 8ST, UK

First Published 2007
© Northumbria University Press 2007

British Library Cataloguing in Publication Data. A Catalogue Record for
this book is available from the British Library.

ISBN 978-1-904794-26-4

The publisher apologises if, inadvertently, any sources remain unacknowledged
and will be glad to make the necessary arrangements at the earliest oportunity.

Designed and printed by External Relations, Northumbria University
Typeset in Adobe Garamond

Northumbria University is the trading name of the
University of Northumbria at Newcastle. NG–253083S/03/09

We would like to dedicate this book
to the memory of Pat Maher, slide librarian and friend.

We would like to thank all the people and organisations
who have helped in the preparation of this book. There are a number
of individuals including Mary and Tom Bromly, Marcus Price
and Ian Caller, who have been particularly helpful. We would also like
to thank the Amber Collective for their contribution and support.

Contents

Part Two
Film and Television

Part Three
Visualising Local Identities

Foreword

   This edited collection developed out of the interests of a group of academics at Northumbria University, who worked together on degree programmes which engaged with visual culture. Because of re-organisation at the University and other factors, many of us no longer work together. Some of the group have moved on to other institutions and roles. Others, including Paul Jones, Peter Beacock and Chris Wharton, have joined the project from other divisions within Northumbria. However, our collective interest in the region's culture and history at a given historical moment, have combined to bring together an account of key aspects of visual culture in a period of enormous social, economic and cultural change. This collection contributes to existing and developing literatures on regional cultures and identities in Britain.

Contributors to the book come from different disciplines: some would describe themselves as visual historians, others cultural theorists. They contribute a range of approaches and styles of writing to the collection and this produces interesting juxtapositions in terms of tone and interpretation. The book, although academic, has also been written in a way that should appeal to a wider readership, particularly those who are interested in the region and its histories. Although there are existing histories of the visual in the North East, most notably *Northumbrian Panorama. Studies in the History and Culture of North East England* (Faulkner (ed.), London: Octavian, 1996), this is the first collection to look specifically at the more recent past. The collection refers to fine art, but much of the focus is on other areas of visual production, the significance of which is sometimes overlooked in general histories. In looking at film alongside design and architecture for instance, we find illuminating connections which give a shape and texture to a reading of the identity of the region in the post-war period.

Introduction

Publicity surrounding Newcastle and Gateshead's bid to become European City of Culture in 2008 inferred a cultural renaissance for the area and the beginning of a new engagement with the visual arts. BALTIC and other galleries which have developed in the wake of the bid certainly represent fresh initiatives in terms of art institutions, and the architectural developments on the Quayside have created an iconic twenty-first century landscape by which the area is widely recognised. However, these developments do not mark some revolutionary change in the relationship of the North East to the visual. The region has had a distinctive and at times groundbreaking history in relation to visual culture for a very long time. The development of art and architecture in the eighteenth and nineteenth century in particular, has been well documented. However we have not had an overview of developments in the post war period in relation to the North East in terms of a broader visual arena. In this collection of chapters we hope to explore some key aspects of visual culture including art, architecture, design, fashion, film and television in the past 60 years, and their significance in a local and wider cultural context.

Newcastle and the surrounding area have gone through many changes since 1945. The blackened industrial city of Newcastle in the early part of the period, which was stereotyped as bleak and depressing has been succeeded in the process of de-industrialisation by an area defined by "party" and "culture". Whilst in the 1950s and 1960s it was the relationship of the North East to the metropolitan which was of most significance in terms of negotiating a cultural identity, in later years the area has been defined in an increasingly international and global context. Geographical, economic and social factors, particularly the process of de-industrialisation, have been critical elements in this process. As well as dislocations at times between the North East and national and international cultural values, we also find dislocations between different areas of visual culture within the region itself. For instance although Newcastle University Fine Art Department had a highly successful national and international profile in the 1960s, with artists Richard Hamilton and Victor Pasmore as key contributors to this, other aspects of visual culture in the region were at some remove from the Zeitgeist. Material culture as represented by fashion and design was slow to connect with new directions in metropolitan style and retailing. The television series *The Likely Lads* and the feature film *Get Carter*, produced in the 1960s and early 1970s respectively, referred in their different ways to a North East still defined by industrial decline and only tentatively engaging with economic, cultural and social change.

The relationship between the industrial past and post-industrial present is a critical element in this collection of chapters. We are also looking at modernity and post-modernity and the ways in which the region has responded and contributed to shifting values in material culture and consumption. In the first section of the book we are looking particularly at architecture and design. Whilst architecture in the post war period has been the subject of a thorough going academic engagement, design has been less well documented despite the region's prominent profile in design education. Architecture, design and the retailing of design have had strong connections with Scandinavian modernism and the geographical identity of the area, remote from London and looking across the North Sea is significant here. Cheryl Buckley in **Taking 'Design' to Newcastle** acknowledges this distinctive relationship. In looking at an exhibition of progressive design promoted by the Design Council and held in Callers Furniture Shop in 1969, she identifies how Newcastle engaged with new ideas and directions in furniture design at the end of the 1960s. Hilary Fawcett's account of fashion retailing and consumption in the region in the 1960s describes how geographical remoteness and economic deprivation resulted in the slow development of new retailing identities for young people in the area in the period. Throughout the 1960s London was the epicentre of fashion and the North East lagged far behind. As with furniture retailing, it wasn't until the end of the decade that Newcastle and the wider North East region began to connect strongly with a 1960s revolution in design and retailing.

Shelagh Wilson in **Art and Design Education in Post-war Newcastle** describes the growing success of fashion design education at the Polytechnic in Newcastle at the end of the 1960s, marking the beginning of a significant contribution from the North East to national and international fashion cultures from the 1970s onwards. Art and design education developed at both Newcastle University and what was latterly to become Northumbria University, to put Newcastle at the vanguard of change in visual education. The success of the Fine Art Department at Newcastle University in the 1950s and 1960s in attracting internationally important artists as teachers and producing graduates who have gone on to have prominent careers is matched by the success of the design courses at Northumbria, in subsequent decades. Jonathan Ive, one of the most internationally successful product designers of the past twenty year's designer of the iMac and iPod is a graduate of Northumbria. There is an irony in the fact that the North East, which has largely failed to develop a new type of industrial infrastructure in the past 30 years, is producing designers whose impact on global markets and contemporary experience is of such massive significance.

In **Changing Urban Landscapes: Architecture and Planning in Newcastle and Gateshead since 1945**, Thomas Faulkner, Paul Jones and Peter Beacock chart the development of the Newcastle from the 1950s, through T. Dan Smith's vision of a Brasilia of the North, into the more recent city landscape, punctuated with the iconic buildings which have contributed to the city's new identity in the twenty-first century. In looking at contemporary Newcastle the authors distinguish the interesting and original from the generic. They identify the Centre for Life, designed by Newcastle University graduate Terry Farrell as offering a distinctive contribution to the city landscape, whilst some other post modern buildings of the past 20 years veer towards a pastiche of historical styles or clichéd predictability.

The second section of the book is concerned with film and television. Peter Hutchings in **Traditions and Transformations: Cinematic Visions of Tyneside** discusses the representation of the area in a range of films across the period. He looks at the North East and its people as depicted both in mainstream cinema as well as in films made locally and on smaller budgets that claim a greater authenticity. James Leggott and Tobias Hochsherf in their chapter, look specifically at Amber Films, a collective based on Newcastle's Quayside. Amber's output from the 1970s onwards has been engaged with social and political issues in an approach informed by left wing politics. In documentary portraits and feature films Amber have contributed to a realist tradition, epitomised in work such as *Shipbuilding*, an elegiac look at a dying industry and the 1987 documentary on local and disgraced politician T. Dan Smith. Feature films such as *Dream On* and *Shooting Magpies* have failed to receive the critical attention which the authors believe they deserve, although with the advent of digital media are now available to a much wider viewing public. The Side Gallery which complements the film culture of Amber with its rich seam of photographs by eminent practitioners such as Sirkka-Liisa Kontinnen and Jimmy Forsyth, is also part of an ideologically informed vision of the area which engages with the experience of North Eastern culture

In a different vein David Martin-Jones examines the representation of the North East in popular television. He discusses the recent use of iconic images of the Angel of the North and the landscape of the Quayside in news reporting and other factual programmes. He also explores the ways in which the region has been represented in series such as Peter Flannery's *Our Friends in the North* and the more recent *55° North*, which have in their different ways articulated aspects of the post-industrial experience. Sarah Leahy in **Visual and Embodied Pleasures: Cinema Going in Newcastle** examines the nature of cinema-going in the region. She looks at audiences and programming with particular reference to the Empire at the Gate, the Tyneside Cinema and the Star and Shadow in Newcastle. She explores the relationship of these cinemas to different cinematic traditions and how they operate in the context of local and national histories and trends.

The third section of the book explores the ways in which representations of North Eastern identity have been contested in recent years by public bodies and institutions. In Paul Usherwood's **Tyneside's "Artistic Renaissance" and Art** he examines the development of the so called visual renaissance in the North East and thinks beyond the Angel of the North, Baltic and Sage, which have almost become clichéd in their ubiquity in the promotion of the area as a centre for the Arts. He sees a vibrant artistic future for the region existing outside the institutionalised arena of the NewcastleGateshead axis, in new developments such as the Star and Shadow Cinema and Art Gallery in the Ouseburn which have a more radical and democratic artistic agenda. Chris Wharton in **The Newcastle Look: Culture as Spectacle** explores the phenomenon of cultural spectacle in Newcastle since 1998, with a particular focus on the use of banners and pennants in Newcastle as a means of defining and promoting the city. As in Paul Usherwood's chapter Chris Wharton sees dislocations between the image of the city as defined by art organisations, business and local government and the reality of the city as lived and experienced by its diverse population.

Paul Barlow in **Tyneside's Modern Rome: The North East's Image of its Roman Past and its Lost Englishness**, examines the ways in which the area's history informs contemporary perceptions of its identity. He examines the significance and representation of Roman history on Tyneside, placing it in the context of a broader history and looks at the ways in which local museums and institutions interpret and differentiate between historical periods. He sees a connection between twenty-first century Newcastle and the visual articulation of Roman history in sites such as Segedunum and Arbeia. Interestingly he claims that, "Far more than mining, shipbuilding, lost Anglo-Saxon kingdoms or any other aspect of its history that is unique to the North East, the modern city seeks to represent itself as the loyal citizenship of the Roman empire, whose newly renewed wall protects it from descent back into irretrievable provincialism".

It could be argued as Paul Barlow suggests that the area sees itself as having moved from a period of provincialism into a present in which Newcastle, the regional capital, is now identified as a vibrant and sophisticated European city. However, as contributors to the book infer, there are discrepancies between the image of the area as now promoted by local institutions and the media, and the reality of a region in which poverty and deprivation remain factors in a patchy recovery from industrial decline. Yet despite social and economic factors, visual culture in the North East has provided a lively source of expression and identity throughout the post war period. Let us hope that it remains so and that we resist being subsumed into a generic and complacent cultural economy in which regional distinctiveness becomes less significant. There is a danger that in opening new Galleries of Modern Art in provincial centres to act as indicators of artistic regeneration, the broader picture and the vitality and quality of what went before is forgotten or ignored. As a region we have an enormous reservoir of talent. Our educational institutions are producing architects, designers, film makers and artists of national and international significance. We have exciting and challenging independent local cultural initiatives. Let us use these resources to shape the area and its experience of visual culture in ways, which while acknowledging wider cultural shifts, keep faith with the history and unique character of this powerfully distinctive place.

Part One

Architecture and Design

Chapter One

—————●●—————

Taking 'Design' to Newcastle

Cheryl Buckley

By focusing on two events in 1969: the opening of the "Design Centre comes to Newcastle" exhibition at Callers furniture shop in March 1969 and the re-opening of the store following a fire in November 1969, this chapter explores a number of key issues in design. Located in the furniture retailers, Callers on Northumberland Street and Saville Row, these two events highlighted the contradictions of design in Britain in the decades following the end of the Second World War. Offering the Newcastle consumer considerable variety in furniture, light fittings, tableware and other domestic products, the Callers furniture shop promoted good form and practical design alongside modernity and innovation, but it also revealed the complexities of design as it engaged not only with approved "good" design, but also pop culture and alternative design practices. As this chapter shows, relatively distant from the metropolitan centre, Callers was nevertheless responsive to the post-war imperative to improve design so as to encourage economic regeneration, but also in tune with the necessity to engage new domestic markets and categories of consumers. Post-war reconstruction in Newcastle, particularly new house building, stimulated the domestic economy by fuelling the demand for consumer goods to create the "ideal home", and retailers such as Callers contributed to this "social reconstruction."

After 1945, two immediate aims were to build a better Britain in the aftermath of war and to underpin economic recovery with strong exports and expanding domestic consumption. Design was important for both. Whilst the development of new manufacturing, management and retailing practices meant that consumption at home and abroad was fore-grounded in the drive to sell new goods, the Welfare State provided a solid foundation for enhanced standards of living that encouraged domestic consumption for both middle-class and working-class consumers. Inextricably linked to a global economy that was dominated by US economic power, the British economy had begun to turn the corner from austerity to growth following $2.7 million of Marshall Aid, and in July 1957 the new Conservative Prime Minister, Harold Macmillan told a Conservative Party rally that most Britons "had never had it so good".[1] With low inflation and unemployment levels, Britain's economy grew from the mid-1950s to the early 1970s. In this context, as people bought their own homes or moved into new or revitalised local authority ones, they looked for new consumer goods to go inside. Those from the working class were starting to buy domestic products – televisions, washing machines, and refrigerators – that before the war had been only available to the affluent classes. Equally, new consumer markets emerged, particularly women and teenagers eager to buy not just domestic products, but personal ones such as fashion, records, and magazines.

In 1951 Seebohm Rowntree's *Poverty and the State* proposed that only 1.6% of the total population earned less than the £5 that defined the poverty line. Additionally, the Welfare State offered tangible and psychological security particularly via house building. Churchill's Conservative government, elected in 1951 – with Harold Macmillan heading the Ministry of Housing – built around 300,000 houses every year from 1953 to 1957. With incentives to builders and subsidies to local authorities, 30% of new homes were private. But some noted that the economy was "based on shaky economic foundations", and by the 1960s there was an increasing awareness that it was not growing as well as economic rivals, particularly Germany and Japan.[2] A new Labour government was elected in 1964 with Harold Wilson at its head, and throughout the remaining years of the decade economic problems dominated, particularly over the value of the pound. This period of economic uncertainty paralleled anxieties over Britain's political status, its position in the Empire and Commonwealth and its world standing. Suez, Kenya, Rhodesia and Cyprus in the 1950s exemplified this.[3]

Society in Britain from the 1950s seemed fundamentally different to that even 20 years earlier, "class differences had softened and class conflict diminished. 'Affluence' had lifted up the whole social pyramid, the pyramid itself was marginally a flatter and more permeable structure".[4] Whilst recognising that social conflict was fragmented, certain areas of conflict exemplified the period. Between young and old, newly arrived immigrants (black and white) and existing communities, men and women, and north and south. Due in part to a serious labour shortage following the war, white European workers, black British citizens, and Irish immigrants came to Britain in large numbers to work in coalmining, agriculture, textiles, domestic service and transport. In a peak year such as 1956, just 30,000 people from the West Indies arrived in Britain in contrast to 60,000 from Ireland, but particular areas of the country experienced changing patterns of settlement.[5]

Women's place in society also attracted a good deal of attention especially following the disruption to roles during wartime. The dilemma for women was how to have full opportunities in life without these being curtailed by patriarchal assumptions about women's role in reproducing the family? Although many more women remained in the workforce after 1945 than after 1918, most were in part-time work. It seemed women wanted to work, but also to have the choice to leave work to have children and to have shorter working hours in order to care for them. Women's work was concentrated in part-time jobs in the embryonic Welfare State and the service sector doing particular types of work "because of profoundly gendered ideas as to what kind of work is appropriate for women".[6] Much of this low paid work was also low status. In tandem with the pull for women to work, albeit in particular types of jobs, was a growing ideology of domesticity evident in women's magazines and reinforced by influential writers such as John Bowlby who highlighted the apparent problem of maternal deprivation in the children of working mothers. In the mid-1950s, 58% of women read magazines, particularly *Woman* and *Woman's Own*, which included features on home, beauty and family. Sales of magazines soared, but "enjoyment of women's magazines [did] not necessarily imply that their readers became solely domestically-oriented fashion slaves".[7] Becoming a woman after 1945 required the on-going negotiation of conflicting desires, expectations and ambitions. Inevitably, the social and political transformations brought by processes of modernity engaged new groups of people – women, young people, the working-class and immigrants – in an on-going dialogue with new design practices that were predominantly modernist in orientation.

As a visual style and as a way of thinking about design and architecture, modernist theories and practices gained in popularity after the Second World War, stimulated in part by the Festival of Britain focused on London's South Bank in 1951. With events and activities across Britain, it offered an opportunity to promote national unity. In addition to arts festivals at Eisteddfod, St David's, Perth, Inverness, Aberdeen, Dumfries and a "Gathering of the Clans" in Edinburgh, the Festival ship, *Campania* (a 16,000 ton escort carrier) took the "Sea Travelling" exhibition to Britain's ports – Newcastle, Bristol, Birkenhead, Southampton, Hull, Plymouth, Dundee, Glasgow, Cardiff and Belfast. A concern with "Britain" rather than "England" marked a progressive and modern approach aiming to extend the wartime spirit of unity and thus chime with the new Labour government's vision of a democratic post-war Britain.[8] The staging of so many regional activities suggested a keen awareness of regionalism, albeit stereotypically depicted via their traditional industries and located within an over-arching concern for national unity.[9] But equally this attempt to recapture the "national community" of wartime could be interpreted as indicative of disintegration and fragmentation as regional economic inequalities came to the fore yet again. The exhibition symbol and poster designed by Abram Games summed this up. Referencing a resurgent Britannia donned in blue, red, and white, Games' poster depicts the United Kingdom as a uniformly green land with no identifiable boundaries except for a coastline marking a clear separation from Europe and the world beyond.[10] Zeal characterised the design processes of the exhibition, and further highlighted the propagandising role of the Council of Industrial Design (COID). Journals such as *Design* magazine (begun in 1949) and the *Things We See* series (published by Penguin in 1947) were vehicles for COID to expound its principles. But for many younger designers and critics the Festival style was anathema. Preferring instead Le Corbusier's *beton brut* or Pop Art, as Banham put it the "modernity" of the exhibition was "old hat".[11] But the impact of various "modernisms" – "Festival Style", Scandinavian, Italian and American – was increasingly evident as the 1950s progressed.

The United States as a centre of modernity was a particular focus, but European and Scandinavian interpretations of modernism provided crucial new perspectives. Scandinavian design re-configured modernist idioms, combining them with indigenous crafts in a manner, which was very appealing to those in Britain searching for modernist languages that took account of natural materials and craft traditions. In contrast, Italian design, visually sophisticated and technologically innovative, appealed to a younger market in particular. Formally adventurous and, not as obviously populist as American product design, both were admired by highbrow consumers and the design intelligentsia, whilst Italian design added stylish sharpness to youth fashion. Young British designers of glass, textiles, ceramics, furniture and lighting responded positively to the new approaches to design seen at the international design fairs in Milan, Stockholm and Copenhagen. The Festival of Britain in 1951 was a showcase for these, but it was also the product of the socially-reformist agenda dominating post-war Britain. The embryonic Welfare State, requiring housing, schools, hospitals and new towns, provided opportunities for those fired by the belief that design could help to construct a better world. This inspired a plethora of pre-war and post-war designers and architects. Exemplary of the modernist desire to use design to build a better world after 1945 was the development of New Towns such as Peterlee in County Durham. From 1948, the pre-war modernist architect Berthold Lubetkin worked there designing one of the North East of England's first new towns, to be succeeded in the mid-1950s, by the then Head of Fine Art at Kings College, Newcastle University, Victor Pasmore. But in parallel there was also an emerging critique of this utopian modernist approach focused on the post-war Institute of Contemporary Art in London and in particular the activities of the Independent Group (this included the writer, critic and architectural historian Reyner Banham, the artists Richard Hamilton and Eduardo Poalozzi, photographer Nigel Henderson, architects Alison and Peter Smithson, and writer Toni del Renzio). Banham was particularly important in articulating this shift in attitudes theoretically as he aligned himself with those looking beyond 1920s European modernism. He was interested in the "second machine age" not the first, even though he was writing comprehensively about the latter in articles in *The Architectural Review* and *Architects' Journal* throughout the 1950s. Unlike the technologies associated with the First Machine Age, these were not just available to an elite, upper middle-class. Instead of looking to Europe for inspiration, Banham turned west towards the United States. American consumer goods fascinated him:

> *Even the man who does not possess an electric razor is likely – in the Westernised world at least – to dispense some previously inconceivable product, such as an aerosol shaving cream, from an equally unprecedented pressurised container, and accept with equanimity the fact that he can afford to throw away, regularly, cutting-edges that previous generations would have nursed for years.*[12]

American mass culture – Hollywood film, literature, advertising, television, automobiles and everyday domestic goods – attracted the attention of the Independent Group as a means of subverting the value systems of "high modernism" and "the conspiracy of good taste" promoted by COID. Avant-garde and elitist in a different way, the Independent Group nevertheless explored the richness and diversity of American popular culture through their practice, writings and exhibitions. Of these, "This is Tomorrow" opening in August 1956 at the Whitechapel Art Gallery was particularly significant. Exhibiting at this were those associated with the Independent Group, who were obsessed with developing "an alternative modernism that engaged with the visual realities and semiotics of contemporary culture".[13] Evident in London in the first instance (Eduardo Paolozzi and Richard Hamilton taught at the Central School of Art and Design in London during the 1950s), the influence of the Independent Group spread to the regions. Hamilton, for example, taught at Newcastle University.

As the Independent Group eulogised about American popular culture, the studio potter Bernard Leach with collaborators, Shoji Hamada and Soetsu Yanagi, toured the United States lecturing at influential art and craft schools – Haystack Mountain School of Craft in Maine and Black Mountain College in North Carolina. They contributed to the development of an aesthetic, which, in celebrating indigenous craft techniques and traditions, marked an alternative response to both modernism and mass cultures in the United States. By the 1960s, some in the craft world perceived Leach's ceramics to be part of a tradition that looked backwards rather than forward, and in this context, studio pottery in

VIEW OF LIVING ROOM
WITH FOLDING DOORS OPEN TO KITCHEN.

Figure 1: Above: 'The House Women Have Chosen', Daily Mail Ideal Home, 1944.

Figure 2: Below: 'A mad mixture of pinks' living room in 'Design Centre comes to Newcastle' exhibition, Callers Furniture Store, Northumberland Street, Newcastle upon Tyne, 1969. Photograph: Ian Caller.

Figure 3: Left: Radical exhibition design by Helen Challen in 'Design Centre comes to Newcastle' exhibition, Callers Furniture Store, Northumberland Street, Newcastle upon Tyne, 1969. Left of photograph, chair in white and gold, student design from Newcastle College of Art and Industrial Design. Photograph: Ian Caller.

Figure 4: Above: Wrighton and Sons Kitchen in orange and white. Dining table and chairs on the right (Robin Day) in 'Design Centre comes to Newcastle' exhibition, Callers Furniture Store, Northumberland Street, Newcastle upon Tyne, 1969. Photograph: Ian Caller.

Figure 5: Below: Lighting department at the rebuilt Callers Furniture Store, 1971. The lighting display was copied from Illums in Copenhagen. Photograph: Pauline Caller.

Britain was increasingly open to new influences from United States West Coast potters such as Peter Voulkos, the work of young British artists, European folk art traditions, and the ceramics of Picasso. British-born ceramicist Ruth Duckworth, taking a sculptural, hand-built approach to ceramics, rejected the dominant Oriental-inspired thrown vessel aesthetic of Leach and moved to the United States to work at the University of Chicago. Duckworth, trained at the Central School, was typical of a new generation of potters in the United Kingdom including Gordon Baldwin, Gillian Lowndes and Ian Auld, who had come through the art schools, particularly the Central School. The Central School produced potters who rejected the dominant Oriental aesthetic, learning instead from the Bauhaus-influenced "Basic Design" approach, which "set out to educate, but not to train".[14] Craft took on new and different meanings in the post-war years, and the establishment of the Crafts Centre in 1946, added to its democratisation as it provided visual complexity in sparse modernist-influenced interiors.

The American home was at the apex of post-war consumer cultures, and in Britain after the mid-1950s it was also the pivotal site for the consumption of new goods (essential for the economy) and in the formulation and representation of a range of ideologies regarding gender, domesticity and the family. In post-1945 Britain, women had a dual responsibility to consume and to reproduce. Thus the *Daily Mail Book of Britain's Post-war Homes* published in 1944 in anticipation of post-war renewal, insisted "housing is a woman's business. She has to make a home of the houses men build".[15] Based on a survey undertaken in 1944, this book purported to represent the ideas and opinions of the "Women of Britain".[16] It described the homes that British women apparently wanted, but at the same time it also exposed the patriarchal assumptions underpinning post-war Welfare State rhetoric. Couched in the language of wartime paternalism, the message was ostensibly about giving women choice and recognising a range of aspirations, albeit within the confines of a home-making role. Women, the survey suggested, were different, and younger women in particular wanted their own washing machines, kitchens and the opportunity to bring up children themselves. The private production of services in the home and the corollary of this, the individual consumption of domestic products seemed to be a cornerstone of women's desires as articulated in this *Daily Mail* survey that aimed to identify the house that women wanted.[17] The essential requirement was for a three bed-roomed house, well-built in a tree-planted cul-de-sac, part of a group but not one of a long repetitive row. In reach of all amenities – shops, churches, health centres, schools and clinics – the house was also to be in close proximity to public transport. With the kitchen over-looking the front of the house and large windows from the sitting and living rooms looking over the garden, the intention was that children could be easily seen as the housewife worked in the home. Interiors and the positioning of services and household technologies were carefully analysed and the kitchen in particular was to be at the epicentre of the future family home. It was rational, planned and equipped with flat, smooth work surfaces to eradicate dirt and dust. This vision of the ideal home was proposed for women across Britain. To coincide with the *Daily Mail* survey an exhibition of "Northern Housing" was staged in Newcastle upon Tyne in December 1944. Organised by the local authorities of Northumberland, Durham, and the North Riding of Yorkshire in collaboration with various government departments, this promoted steel factory-made houses as a solution to the impending housing crisis. Housing schemes, model homes and interiors proposed by several local Urban District Councils included the South Bank Housing Scheme at Eston in the North Riding of Yorkshire, the Longbenton Housing estate from Newcastle Corporation, and a model kitchen from Stockton on Tees Corporation. The gas industry promoted "The Practical Northern Home", designed by Mary Proctor Cahill ARIBA (of the Alnwick firm, Reavell and Cahill). This particular home, aimed at "the great masses of people who may be said to be of moderate means", was declared "practical for North of England conditions in every sense of the word".[18] Cahill proposed flexibility with a dining recess off the kitchen so as to ameliorate the "isolation sometimes felt when the kitchen is entirely [a] workshop".[19] Implicit in such literature was the idea that women architects had a particular aptitude in certain fields of design. Designing public sector housing, schools, and hospitals for local authorities reinforced patriarchal notions of women's roles, but conversely it offered women opportunities in these fields.[20]

The home in post-war Britain became a vital space for the representation of modern design, but it also offered a new generation of architects and designers the opportunity to produce appropriate housing plans, desirable products, and stylish furniture for home consumption. In a number of ways, it was in the home that the post-war modernist vision of a better world was best articulated and in which the integration of design – architecture, crafts, interiors, products, and furniture – most effectively achieved. In the aftermath of the 1951 Festival of Britain, the COID had consolidated its position as arbiter of "good" design in Britain. As part of the exhibition, it had drawn up a stock list of over 20,000 "exhibition worthy" products of British industry. With this, its index of industrial designers, and via its mouthpiece, *Design* magazine, its authority in defining standards and values in design in the United Kingdom was assured.[21] By 1956 it had also opened the Design Centre in London as a permanent exhibition space for well designed goods. These designs codified the simplified and restrained post-war modernism preferred by the Council, but by the end of the 1950s, its determination to assess and prioritise what was important in design was being questioned by consumer representatives and undermined by a growing perception that it was indicative of a "narrow middle-class taste".[22] Nevertheless between March and April 1969, it set about educating and directing the taste of the inhabitants of Newcastle upon Tyne with an exhibition "The Design Centre Comes to Newcastle" in the furniture store, Callers situated in the city's premier shopping area, Northumberland Street and adjacent Saville Row.

Founded in the early 1920s by Abe Caller, the son of an East European Jewish cabinet-maker who had set up business in Newcastle in 1897, Callers was one of a number of established furniture retailers in Newcastle upon Tyne (others included Chapmans and Robsons).[23] By 1938, Callers had moved from New Bridge Street to 54 Northumberland Street into premises previously occupied by the Townsend Gallery, specialists in china and glass.[24] Refurbished in 1954–55, the shop frontages and showrooms in Northumberland Street and Saville Row were distinctively modern.[25] The façade in particular had a sharp, geometric look with black vitrolite surfaces, red plastic lettering and the "Callers" name on a fascia in pink neon tubing.[26] Following the death of their father in 1958, Roy and Ian Caller took over the day-to-day management of the family-owned company. Like their father, they bought from well-regarded manufacturers in High Wycombe such as Ercol Furniture Ltd (established in 1920 by Lucian Ercolani) and E Gomme Ltd, (Donald Gomme designed the G-Plan range in the mid 1950s), Harold Lebus in London and Meredew in Letchworth, but they were also "intrigued by modern design".[27] In particular they liked the simplicity, modernity, and quality of Scandinavian modern design especially that from Denmark. Regularly visiting the Copenhagen Furniture Fair and sourcing the goods on display for their own Newcastle shop, they also admired the interior design and products of Illums, one of Copenhagen's foremost department stores.[28] Increased business with Denmark led to the appointment of an agent there, but not only did Roy and Ian Caller import modern Danish design, they also borrowed display ideas from European stores. One innovation was the Christmas window display – initially seen in Parisian stores such as Gallerie Lafayette – they introduced this to promote the company name and to stimulate consumer interest over the trade's normally sluggish Christmas period. Another device was the establishment of a gallery of model rooms. These were extremely innovative. In displaying "ideal" rooms that incorporated furniture, textiles, lighting, ceramics, glass and even "art", Callers guided relatively inexperienced consumers of modern design as they put together their "modern" homes.[29] Callers partnership with the COID to bring the Design Centre to Newcastle was indicative of their enthusiasm for modern design, although it is worth remembering that Roy and Ian Caller were already experienced furniture retailers with extensive knowledge of the furniture trade and design.

The COID appointed the architect/designer Helen Challen to design the exhibition, and Ian Caller recalled the battle of wills as he and his brother toned down her radical ideas for a North-East market. With the construction of six fully furnished rooms (including a kitchen) as well as other displays, exemplary modern design was shown at the "Design Centre comes to Newcastle" exhibition over four weeks in the spring of 1969. Bringing progressive 1960s design to Northern consumers, an advertisement for the exhibition in the Newcastle *Evening Chronicle* claimed "this exhibition enables Newcastle shoppers to choose from a considerable variety of well-designed modern furniture".[30] With a heading "Why not a Chair of Paper or Foam," consumers were invited to come and see Frederick Scott's foam seating for Hille, David Bartlett's slot-together paper chair "costing little over £2," and Quasar Khanh's clear plastic inflatable chair. Other exhibits included Harry Bertoia's sculptural metal basket chairs, Peter Murdoch's hexagonal plastic chairs, stools and low tables for Hille, knockdown furniture for children as well as Fidelity radios and Philips automatic washing machines. Announcing "what London has today Newcastle has as well…", the "Trend" section of the *Newcastle Journal* gave positive encouragement to modern design, and emphasised the importance of the Design Centre as a "must-be-seen" place in London.[31] Under a photo of a living room, the caption read "A mad mixture of pinks – from sugar to shocking – plus a dash of midnight blue, a splash of purple and a lot of orange…overstated, but deliberately so".[32] The intention was "not to copy a room-setting inch by dramatic inch, but to pick up the odd idea, select the odd design, maybe pinch a colour scheme".[33] Rebutting the question, "All for show?" it confirmed that "all furniture, curtaining and accessories will be on sale in Newcastle".[34] The reporter for the *Newcastle Journal* was generally enthusiastic, particularly liking the room-setting displays in which the COID's mainly modernist principles were most apparent. In the bed-sitting room for a teenager, for example, "careful design" enabled the room to look twice its size, whereas the award-winning "International" fitted kitchen range by Wrighton & Sons from

1968 was promoted as rational efficient design, but available in vibrant orange as well as white, it pointed to the impact of pop culture in the later 1960s. Lit by spotlights, "streamlined", and based on a 10cm module rather than the British Imperial measurements, it was extremely forward-looking. Incorporated in this were the latest electrical appliances including a split-level hob and oven, top-loader washing machine, electric kettle and toaster. The overall look of the living and sitting rooms was abstract and bold with bright printed textiles and rugs, fitted shelving, low horizontal sofas, and made from new materials.

Opened by Sir Paul Reilly and with an accompanying lecture to architects and designers at the Northumberland St store by Gordon Russell, education was a dominant theme of the Design Centre exhibition – both for the consumer and designer. Alongside the Design Council exhibits were prototypes by students of the Newcastle College of Art and Industrial Design. Several of these revealed the students' knowledge of recent trends in furniture and hinted at the widening gap between the paternalistic approach of the COID and 1960s pop culture as was hinted at in Russell's lecture. (Upon being questioned about the apparent draughtiness of an exemplary modernist bus shelter that he had used to illustrate his lecture, Russell's own class perspective came to the surface as he replied that as this audience rarely took the bus, it wasn't a serious concern.)[35] In the advertisement for the exhibition in *Evening Chronicle*, a number of points were emphasised that point up the COID's priorities: firstly the promotion of "Britishness" via British-made goods; secondly, the importance of goods being "designed" by designers, thus names were prominent – textiles by Margot Shore and seating by Frederick Scott, Harry Bertoia, William Plunkett, and Robin Day; and thirdly, the insistence on design standards denoted by the Design Centre "kite" symbol. Nevertheless, the throwaway and disposable chairs, as well as vivid colours and vibrant patterns were harbingers of the impact of pop cultures and the needs of new markets that were to be comprehensively addressed in the re-built shop.

Seven months after the exhibition (in November 1969), catastrophe struck Callers as an electrical fault completely burned down the shop. Rebuilt to a design by the brothers' cousin Peter Caller, it opened in 1971 with a plethora of new design features and, just as importantly, new sections.[36] Without shareholders to assuage, the brothers could develop in ways that appealed to them alone; in 1963 in response to the inept service that they had received from an established travel company, (aimed at the upper-end of the market), they had launched their own travel agency (within the furniture store) to provide affordable "package holidays" abroad for more cost-conscious consumers. Such an awareness of new markets was also evident in the re-furbished shop as a record department was opened. Planned to bring in the youth market, as there were limited record shops in Newcastle, it was located adjacent to the electrical department, and proved a spectacular success from the outset. The interior design of the reconstructed store was flamboyant and specific features (brick curved wall and glass floor) were borrowed directly from the Copenhagen store, Illums.[37] Open plan with brick, steel and glass, internal water features, and themed rooms; the store was an example of modern design in Newcastle that aimed to appeal to a range of markets. The stunning lighting department – more akin to abstract sculpture than a retailing display – was again inspired by Illums, but it brought a visual sophistication to the increasingly difficult business of selling furniture. Roy and Ian Caller were sharply attuned to the changes in the furniture trade, but they remained relatively up-beat, aiming to provide furniture and domestic goods for the burgeoning middle-class and working-class consumers of Newcastle upon Tyne.[38] They understood that the didacticism of the COID would not work: for example, although they were happy to display Russell furniture, they knew it would not sell well as it was too expensive and inappropriate for their predominantly lower middle-class and working class markets. Equally, Callers' displays showed an awareness of the disposable or futuristic aesthetic associated with the Independent Group, but they were a far cry from the radical avant-gardism epitomised by Alison and Peter Smithson's House of the Future designed in the mid-1950s. Working collaboratively since graduating from Newcastle University in the late 1940s, the Smithsons' design offered an alternative vision of a technological future envisaged 25 years hence. Predominantly the work of Alison Smithson, this "gadget-filled dream of the middle-income household" was made of a type of plastic capable of mass-production in a single unit, and it included a self-cleaning bath, easy-to-clean corners, and remote controls for the television and lighting.[39] But firmly rooted in the competitive retailing marketplace of Newcastle upon Tyne, Callers offered instead an array of desirable domestic products – modern and traditional – that provided essential furnishings for various "Ideal Homes" typically comprising three-bedrooms, living and dining rooms, and a kitchen. New-house building had gathered pace in post-war Newcastle. A key element of its 1963 Development Plan was the development of around 25,000 new houses and the revitalisation of 12,000 others. In addition several New Towns were built within the region.[40] On Newcastle's outskirts were Cramlington, Killingworth and Washington New Town, and within travelling distance in County Durham were Newton Aycliffe and Peterlee. Not only did Callers have branches in Blaydon, Morpeth, Consett,

Hebburn, South Shields and Ponteland, but also in Washington New Town and as far south as Middlesborough, so as to capture regional markets. As new homes needed new categories of goods as well as traditional ones, Callers was on hand to guide relatively inexperienced consumers in their domestic purchases.

Newcastle remained economically "fragile" during the post-war period mainly due to the processes of de-industrialisation that gathered pace. Disguising this was its dramatic growth as a regional retailing centre, which saw retailing turnover in the central shopping area of Newcastle (focused on Northumberland Street), increase from £56m to £121m between 1951 and 1971.[41] Large retailers such as Marks and Spencer, Littlewood, British Home Stores, Woolworth, Burton, and the department stores Fenwick, Bainbridge and Binns catered for the new categories of goods desired by the post-war consumer. Smaller independent companies sold up, diversified, or moved location. Several had already moved from Northumberland St – Chapmans, for example, had sold their Northumberland Street shop to Marks and Spencer in the mid-1930s. But as this chapter has shown, Callers retained its place on Newcastle's premier shopping street due to an astute understanding of new and shifting markets, its eclectic offering of "Scandinavian" design, Pop culture, and traditional "British" furniture and domestic goods, and the willingness of Roy and Ian Caller to operate in an independent manner. In 1984, the company sold their valuable Northumberland Street lease and concentrated on the travel agency business.

Notes

1. Schenk, C.R. (1994) 'Austerity and Boom', in Johnson, P. (ed.) *20th Century Britain. Economic, Social and Cultural Change.* Essex: Longmans, p.309.
2. Madgwick, P. J., Seeds, D. & Williams, L.J. (1982) *Britain since 1945.* London: Hutchinson, p.13.
3. Madgwick, P. J., Seeds, D. & Williams, L.J. (1982) *Britain since 1945.* London: Hutchinson, p.13.
4. Madgwick, P. J., Seeds, D. & Williams, L.J. (1982) *Britain since 1945.* London: Hutchinson, p.35.
5. Kushner. T. (1994) *'Immigration and "Race Relations" in Postwar British Society'*, in Johnson, P. (ed.) *20th Century Britain. Economic, Social and Cultural Change.* Essex: Longmans, p.413.
6. Lewis, J. (1992) *Women in Britain since 1945.* Oxford: Blackwell, p.68.
7. Thane, P. (1994) *'Women Since 1945', in Johnson, P. (ed.) 20th Century Britain. Economic, Social and Cultural Change.* Essex: Longmans, p.400.
8. Conekin, B.E. (2003) *'The autobiography of a nation'. The 1951 Festival of Britain.* Manchester: Manchester University Press, p.10.
9. Massey, A. (1995) The Independent Group. *Modernism and mass culture in Britain, 1945-1959.* Manchester: Manchester University Press, p.10.

10. Conekin, B.E. (2003) 'The autobiography of a nation'. *The 1951 Festival of Britain*. Manchester: Manchester University Press, p.131.

11. Banham, M. & Hillier, B. (1976) *A Tonic to the Nation*. The Festival of Britain 1951. London: Thames and Hudson, p.193.

12. Banham, R. (1960) *Theory and Design in the First Machine Age*. London: Architectural Press, p.9.

13. Stephens, C. & Stout, K. (eds.) (2004) *Art & the 60s. This Was Tomorrow*. London: Tate, p.10.

14. Harrod, T. (1999) *The Crafts in Britain in the 20th Century*. New Haven, CT: Yale University Press, p.232.

15. Pleydell-Bouverie, M.F. (1944) *Daily Mail Book of Britain's Post-war Homes*. London, p.12

16. Pleydell-Bouverie, M.F. (1944) *Daily Mail Book of Britain's Post-war Homes*. London, p.23.

17. Pleydell-Bouverie, M.F. (1944) *Daily Mail Book of Britain's Post-war Homes*. London, p.87.

18. Leaflet, Northern Housing exhibition, December 1-30, 1944, Baths Hall, Northumberland Road, Newcastle upon Tyne, p.8.

19. Leaflet, The Gas Industry Presents.... *"The Practical Northern Home"*, 1944.

20. Walker, L. (1984) *Women Architects. Their Work*. London: Sorella Press, p.19.

21. Banham, M. & Hillier, B. (1976) *A Tonic to the Nation*. The Festival of Britain 1951. London: Thames and Hudson, p.60.

22. Woodham, J. (1997) *Twentieth-century Design*. Oxford: Oxford University Press, p.190.

23. Author interview with Ian Caller, 21 December 2006.

24. Ward's Directory, 1938.

25. Plans T186/15642, Tyne and Wear Museums Archive.

26. Plans T186/15642, Tyne and Wear Museums Archive.

27. Author interview with Ian Caller, 21 December 2006.

28. Author interview with Ian Caller, 21 December 2006.

29. Author interview with Ian Caller, 21 December 2006.

30. 'Why not a Chair of Paper or Foam?', Newcastle Evening Chronicle, March 21, 1969, p.9.

31. 'Design Centre Comes North', *Newcastle Journal*, March 20, 1969, p.6.

32. 'Design Centre Comes North', *Newcastle Journal*, March 20, 1969, p.6.

33. 'Design Centre Comes North', *Newcastle Journal,* March 20, 1969, p.6.

34. 'Design Centre Comes North', *Newcastle Journal*, March 20, 1969, p.6.

35. Author interview with Ian Caller, 21 December 2006.

36. Author interview with Ian Caller, 21 December 2006.

37. Author interview with Ian Caller, 21 December 2006.

38. Author interview with Ian Caller, 21 December 2006.

39. Sadler, S. (2004) '*British Architecture in the Sixties*', in Stephens, C. & Stout, K. (eds.) *Art & the 60s. This Was Tomorrow*. London: Tate, p.131, and '*Design at the Design Museum: Alison and Peter Smithson*'. Available at: http://www.designmuseum.org/design/index (Accessed: 10 September 2005).

40. For a fuller discussion see Faulkner, T.E. (2001), '*Architecture in Newcastle*', in Colls, R. & Lancaster, W. (eds) Newcastle upon Tyne. *A Modern History*. Chicester, Sussex: Phillimore; and Byrne, D. (2001) '*The Reconstruction of Newcastle: planning since 1941*', in Colls, R. & Lancaster, W. (eds) Newcastle upon Tyne. *A Modern History*. Chicester, Sussex: Phillimore.

41. Vall, N. (2001) 'The Emergence of the Post-Industrial Economy in Newcastle 1914-2000', in Colls, R. & Lancaster, W. Newcastle upon Tyne. A Modern History. Chicester, Sussex: Phillimore, p.66.

Chapter Two

"We Gotta Get Out of This Place": Fashion, Gender and Identity in the North East in the 1960s

Hilary Fawcett

In this chapter, I will examine the ways in which the North East of England began to engage with the fashion revolution of the 1960s, and how young people and especially young women in the region, experienced the process of fashioning with its pleasures and frustrations. In exploring this material I am challenging the totalising approaches of the majority of texts on 1960s fashion, which focus predominantly on London, and exclude the ways in which fashion cultures developed outside the capital. The recent and successful fashion exhibition *The Swinging Sixties*, held at the Victoria and Albert Museum reinforced a London-centric reading of the period (Breward, Lister and Gilbert, 2006). Commonly received perceptions about the "look" of the 60s are based on iconography from the dominant London-based media. Images of Carnaby Street, Jean Shrimpton, Mary Quant, *Ready Steady Go*, etc. represent a highly finished and stylised fashion culture and are constantly used and re-used in contemporary reference. They are consistently offered as evidence of the supposedly classless new world for young people in the 1960s, in which self definition in terms of style offered possibilities of social movement and a new enfranchisement in a glossy consumer culture. This is a highly questionable premise and far from a universal given. For many young people across the country, an engagement with a bright new consumer world in which they were supposed to play a central part was largely illusory in the first half of the 1960s.

Liverpool and other regional cities have been identified as significant in the so called "youth revolution" of the 1960s, and said to represent a growing de-centralisation in terms of cultural innovation, but their importance lay in developments in popular music rather than in the areas of style, design or fashion. Liverpudlian performers such as the Beatles and Cilla Black, who perhaps surprisingly given her "mumsy" image was highly fashionable in the 1960s,[1] were styled in London for international success. Eric Burdon of The Animals, the group referred to as the Newcastle Sound, has spoken of his discomfort at being dressed in Carnaby Street "gear" for the release of single *The House of the Rising Sun* in 1963. He disliked the experience of being packaged in sixties style metropolitan fashion, preferring the group's original image which connected strongly to the uncompromising nature of their approach to Rhythm and Blues and paid little truck to changing fashion mores in representing the still relatively stylistically disengaged identity of young men in the Newcastle area.

In examining the development of fashion markets and experience of fashioning particularly for young women in the North East in the 1960s, I am using autobiography, as well as cultural and social history. I was born in 1949 so my growing up was done in the 1960s. I spent from 1960 until 1967 living with my parents in the suburbs of Sunderland, where I attended the local convent school and led a life typical in many ways of that generation of young women who were the first from working class and lower middle class backgrounds to aspire to higher education. In 1967 I left home to study Fine Art at Newcastle University, a short distance from my home geographically but a world away in reality from my provincial upbringing. This chronological schism in terms of my experience fitted rather neatly in the context of wider cultural change, as is represented in the high modernity of the period from 1963 to 1967 and the increasingly post-modern and eclectic late 1960s. My own experience of fashion, fashioning and femininity in the period up to 1967, was one in which I was essentially locked into the local fashion market with its deprivations and frustrations in relation to the metropolitan ideal. During my time at University however, I entered a more sophisticated culture where an engagement with a metropolitan stylishness and cool was a prerequisite for social and even academic success. It was also a period at the end of the 1960s when cities such as Newcastle began to engage more fully with changing trends in fashion retailing.

My earliest memory of fashion culture was of accompanying my mother to Binns Department Store in Fawcett Street, where we would have afternoon tea in the restaurant whilst in-store fashion models would promenade in clothes by manufacturers such as Susan Small, Dereta or Hebe Sports. This was very much a shared and pleasurable experience and so fashion for me began to represent an arena of escape from the mundane world of school and suburban Sunderland life in the grey post-war 1950s. My mother was much concerned with issues of good and bad taste. My maternal grandmother, like many working class women in the period, had been in service at the home of aristocratic landowners in the 1920s and 1930s and imbibed values about class and taste which informed my mother's view of the world of fashion. Indeed my mother's favourite word to describe clothes of which she approved was that they were "classy". This meant a modernist aesthetic of subtle colours and understatement, as had been exemplified in the 1940s by the royal icon Princess Marina of Kent and would later to be represented par excellence by the designs of Mary Quant.[2] As a child I was not allowed to wear the American influenced plastic sandals or fluorescent socks favoured by many of my friends and was dressed in tweed and camel coats and Start-rite shoes, in emulation of the Royal children, Charles and Anne.

These attitudes to clothes and status seem invidious now in a period when fashion is essentially generic and celebrities such as Colleen McLaughlin and Jade Goody wear the same style clothes as aristocrats and princesses, as well as the average girl on the street. In the 1950s however when Richard Hoggart *et al.* opposed the Americanisation of British culture and Nancy Mitford was concerned with what was "U" and "non U", prejudice and snobbery in relation to taste and style were common place.[3] Perhaps this was represented most emphatically in the attitudes of part of the lower middle class whose own status had been hard and recently won. Suburban life was marked by concerns about good and bad taste. In the 1950s consumer culture began to escalate and institutions such as the Design Council were proscriptive on these issues, even the popular press engaged in debates on issues of taste. Many homeowners defined their status through consumption and identification with established middle class values in taste, which could distinguish them from the working class majority. In Sunderland in the 1950s working people were being moved from nineteenth century urban housing to the proliferation of council estates in which they were to be ghettoised under the paternalistic ethos of post war planning. Class distinction was endorsed by the planners, reinforcing existing divisions in the post-war community.

The Regional and the Metropolitan

In the late 1950s and early 1960s Sunderland was a town economically dependent on the industries of shipbuilding and coalmining. It was architecturally and commercially inferior to neighbouring Newcastle, but it still had a handsome town centre dominated by a Victorian library and the imposing central conduit of Fawcett Street. Women's fashion was obviously present but not massively articulated in retail markets in Sunderland in the later 1950s. It was a period in which High Street fashion was still in a tentative revival after the Second World War and the pressures of clothes rationing which hadn't ended until the early 1950s.[4] Young women and some older women engaged in fashionable types of dress, but hard work and thrift were still writ large and the most colourful adult clothes that I remember were worn by Teddy Boys in local mining villages-dandy pitmen who paraded their drape jackets on Sundays on the way to the pub.

Issues of class and region in terms of fashion identities are sometimes difficult to differentiate when looking at the turn of the decade. The austerity of the immediate post-war period in terms of fashion was still very evident up to the late 1950s and this was a national rather than regional issue. In the documentary film by Karl Reiz *We are the Lambeth Boys*,[5] made in London on the cusp of the 1960s we see teenage working class young men and women congregating at a youth club in London's East End. The girls wear predominantly homemade or cheap high street clothes. Their hair is poorly cut, shoes scuffed, there is an unfinished quality to their appearance and an apparent naivety in their behaviour. These are young women living in London, soon to be heralded the centre of the fashion world. They are massively removed however, by both economic strictures and cultural awareness, from the radical chic of early Mary Quant, who was at this point dressing Chelsea girls in clear anticipation of 60s cool, or from the embryonic mod culture which was developing in the north of the City. Here on the cusp of the 1960s class and economic factors are more significant than regional identity in terms of young people's engagement with developing fashion markets.

By the early 1960s, the North East's geographical remoteness had become highly significant in a growing distance between patterns of fashion retailing in the region and the rapidly changing youth orientated metropolitan market. London saw a revolution in terms of fashion for young people predicated on a constantly changing dynamic led by new designers and entrepreneurs, and responsive to the style of mod culture and the growing economic power of teenagers. Travel to London from the North East was expensive, few people owned cars and consumers were dependent on the local fashion market which lagged significantly behind. It was through the media that information about the new developments in fashion and popular culture were disseminated to regional consumers. Magazines played a critical role in the lives of young women and although it is difficult to establish sales figures for young people's magazines in the 1960s on a regional basis, issues of class, taste and aspiration informed the consumer profile popular literature available in the early 1960s.

Honey, the best known new teenage magazine of the period was first published in 1963 and was revolutionary in providing young women with their own stylish and glossy periodical. However, it was metropolitan in tone, at the cutting edge of fashion and prohibitively expensive for many who may have been still at school or in poorly paid jobs at its inception. There were well-established and cheaper teen magazines such as *Boyfriend* and *Roxy*, which had a largely working class and lower middle class readership, and were still promoting a stylistically compromised identity in terms of fashion for young women until the mid sixties. Even as late as 1964 *Boyfriend* was presenting an image for young women who appears frumpish and vaguely middle aged. Because of the small number of relatively cheap magazines at the beginning of the 60s many teenage girls, including myself, also read copies of their mother's *Woman* and *Woman's Own*, the best selling weekly magazines of the period. These offered sewing patterns and knitting patterns as a cheaper alternative to bought clothes and a construction of femininity and attractiveness which was predicated on traditional ideas of romance and domesticity. The fashion content of these cheaper teenage and adult magazines related more closely to the fashion retail market of Fawcett Street in Sunderland or Littlewoods' Catalogue than the Kings Road or Carnaby Street. It represented a significant contrast to the sophisticated constructions of femininity and style to be found in *Honey* and its cheaper but still metropolitan sister, *Petticoat*. The gap between these two magazine cultures was to become a yawning chasm as the decade progressed *(see Figure 1)*.

Fashion Retailing in the North East in the mid-1960s

In Sunderland's retail centre in 1964 we find a limited set of options in relation to affordable fashion for young people. The department store Binns, which had been taken over by The House of Frazer in the 1950s, had expanded in 1962 and was the most significant retail outlet in the town. There were other department stores including Joplings, Blacketts and Liverpool House, but these were essentially conservative in their approach to fashion. National chains such as Marks & Spencer and British Home Stores, provided moderately priced staples for a range of ages. Marks & Spencer had lowered its prices in the 1950s, and between 1956 and 1966 had doubled its share of the British clothing market. Rachel Worth claims that Marks & Spencer "saw itself at the vanguard of fashion in some respects in this period" (Worth, 2007: 127), but for young people it still represented a largely conventional and unexciting store. There were a number of dress shops for older women in the town including Paige and Eve Brown but the most upmarket and expensive were Deftys and Books in Holmside, which catered for an older market, albeit a more glamorous one than many of its competitors. Home dressmaking even into the mid-1960s was still the only way that some of the ideas represented in new fashion cultures could be realised.

My own increasing interest in fashion was inspired in part by my childhood deprivations in terms of popular style but also represented a resistance to the world of study and moral responsibility in which I found myself. My mother's engagement with notions of taste and its implications in terms of social status meant that I also aspired to achieve a degree of distinction in my own appearance.

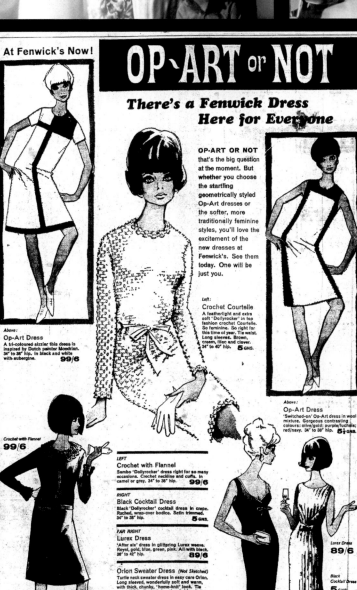

Figure 1: Above Left: The author and friends at the age of 15 in Sunderland, 1964.

Figure 2: Left: Newspaper advert for Fenwicks Newcastle, 1964.

Figure 3: Above Right: Downbeat Club, early 1960s. Photograph: Jim Perry.

*Figure 4: Above: Window of Marcus Price,
Percy Street, mid 1960s. Photograph:
Marcus Price.*

Figure 5: Left: Image from Honey,
March 1969.

Frank Mort speaks of the "history of commercial society in Britain... in the 1950s and 1960s (displaying) an increasing trend towards the self-dramatisation of identity" (Mort, 1997: 29). My own desire for originality in terms of image was part of this shift from the "mass" to the stylishly individual. However Sunderland's poverty of choice in fashion deprived me of the opportunities I needed to transform myself and even trips to Newcastle offered few interesting and affordable options. Photographs of Newcastle in the 1960s present a blackened and still heavily industrial city, despite its elegant Grainger and Dobson centre. Even in the late 60s the terrain of *Get Carter* and *The Likely Lads* (see Hochscherf and Leggott) was one of depressing "back to backs", with the occasional high rise and fly-over punctuating the sky line courtesy of T. Dan Smith. For me and many others at that time, who lived in the wide conurbation beyond the city, Newcastle represented something grand and exciting. However an article entitled "Teenagers can be smart and 'with it' too" by Elizabeth Scotson in the *Newcastle Journal* in January 1964, promoted a very dated looking suit with a box pleated skirt priced at £7 from Joplings, Sunderland as a fashion solution for teenage girls. This was proposed as an alternative to "dirty duffle coats and black stockings". It seemed that the concept of 1960s teenage style was still struggling to be established in the North Eastern consciousness.

In terms of retailing Newcastle had distinct limitations. In 1964 the major shopping area was in and around Northumberland Street, where there were Books Fashions, C&A Modes and Etam. Shoe shops dominated much of Northumberland Street, but not the likes of the new London-based Ravel or Raoul but Barrett, Saxone, Manfields and Freeman Hardy Willis. The department store Fenwicks was on Northumberland Street and it and Bainbridge's, which was on Grainger Street, were major players in Newcastle's retail profile. Much has been written about the role of department stores in the democratisation of fashion, but in London new styles of fashion marketing and retailing were challenging the long established position of the department store as a leader in the promotion of popular fashion on the High Street. Bill Lancaster discusses the competition between the Newcastle department stores Binns, Fenwicks and Bainbridges in the early 1960s and the concerns about the supremacy of Fenwicks given its key position on Northumberland Street (Lancaster, 1995: 197-198). However, it wasn't until the late 1960s that these stores experienced any significant challenge from new retailing styles in Newcastle.

In 1964 Fenwicks began to sell Quant's "Ginger Group" collection, in a very tentative attempt to engage with the developing fashion Zeitgeist and there was an excited response to this development in the fashion page of the local paper. Advertisements for Fenwicks in the mid-1960s showed an engagement with changing fashion trends in the promotion of labels such as Dollyrocker, which brought a rather watered down version of high fashion to the wider market. In 1964 we find a copy of Yves Saint Laurent's Mondrian dress advertised in an "Op meets Pop" spread in the *Evening Chronicle* and later in the decade Ossie Clarke by Radley and Jeff Banks were two of a number of well-known and relatively expensive fashion labels available in store (*see Figure 2*). Looking at fashion advertising in the Newcastle *Chronicle* in 1964 C&A, the Dutch owned clothing retailer, was by far the most interesting, incorporating stylized drawings of "fashion dollies" which perhaps exaggerated the trendiness of the clothes on sale. C&A, however, was one of the very few relatively fashionable and affordable sources of clothes for young women in the city at this time.

Shops which are remembered as having an exotic appeal in the city were Lyktan in Shakespeare Street and the Stone Gallery in Brunswick Place. These shops sold jewellery and so were tangential to fashion, but represented a distinctive approach to style in what was still an unsophisticated retailing economy. Lyktan specialized in Scandinavian design, including highly expressive Marameko textiles from Finland and Swedish and Danish jewellery. The Stone Gallery interesting and arty greetings cards alongside Scandinavian silver and stainless steel jewellery. This type of modernist design is most frequently associated with the 1950s but its significance lasted long into the 1960s and particularly in a city such as Newcastle which was removed from some of the more revolutionary aspects of 60s style. Interestingly Thomas Faulkner, Paul Jones and Peter Beacock and Cheryl Buckley in their respective chapters refer to the persistence of Scandinavian Modernism in architecture and design in the North East, after its influence had subsided nationally. Our Eastern seaboard has made the area one in which influences from the Baltic and Scandinavia continued to have a strong impact deep into the twentieth century.

An epiphanic moment in terms of my own experience of fashion came on a family visit to London in 1964 when I discovered Wallis Shops. The Wallis chain had started in the 1920s and had been transformed by Jeffrey Wallis, in the post-war period from a rather downmarket rag trade enterprise into a dynamic fashion business. He was inspired by Lady Rendelsham's boutique selling French Ready to Wear in Carnaby Street and his pick of Paris Collections made Parisian fashion accessible in well made and not exorbitantly priced copies. As a designer manufacturer he made a distinctive and often under regarded contribution to the development of British fashion retailing for younger women in the 1960s. My first experience of Wallis was on walking down Kensington High Street towards Harrods and being enchanted by the Wallis shop window. I bought two much cherished dresses which I wore for a number of years. A year later to my delight a Wallis franchise opened in Binns in Sunderland, allowing for a distinctive but not necessarily London led source of innovatively designed and well made clothes for young women. Binns in Newcastle also had a franchise. Wallis made up-to-the-minute copies of French designers Chanel, Yves San Laurent and Emmanuelle Kahn available in the remote North East. Interestingly it was a French influence rather than British cutting edge fashion styling that played one of the more significant roles in developing fashion retailing for young women in the North East in the mid-1960s.

Fashion and Popular Culture

The fashioning of young women, indeed young people in this period, was also influenced by popular cultural identities outside that of fashion itself. Angela McRobbie has discussed the ways in which young women in particular, often marginalized in subcultures, found new identities for themselves in developing consumer cultures (McRobbie, 1980). The Folk Revival was one such culture and it was a site in which a constituency of young women could identify new types of femininity informed by ideological change as well as musical fashion. The Folk Revival had been a very strong part of the music scene in London in the very early 1960s but had a particular and long lasting significance in the North East, just as it did in towns like Hull and Liverpool. It was also the case that many night clubs in the North East were distinctly adult until the later 60s and folk clubs offered younger teenagers an accessible recreational experience. The folk scene brought with it a new set of female iconographies from America. Joan Baez and Mary Travers from Peter, Paul and Mary, were two key figures whose style lay between Beat and Hippie and were easily imitated. This allowed young women to customise basic clothes to create something which was not tied to a highly fashionable market but could be created cheaply. I combined my small Wallis wardrobe with items from more mundane sources like Marks & Spencer. This identity also had a softer more romantic feel than dominant fashion iconographies of the mid sixties, which might be described as High Pop. This sensibility tied more coherently to the experience of young women from backgrounds such as my own, whose femininity was conditioned by reading *Jane Eyre* and *Little Women* and whose sensibility in their earlier teens was at odds with the dominant sexualized swinging chick, as identified by John Crosby and located in London.[6]

Interestingly despite the dislocations between fashion in London and other regions, live music by the most innovative of bands was consistently available on a circuit, which included night clubs, dance halls and college and university hops. Clubs in places as remote from the metropolis as South Shields would have bands such as the Yardbirds performing straight from gigs at London's Marquee or Flamingo. The bands brought with them the most up-to-date of clothes and their stylishness would often be at odds, certainly in the earlier 1960s, with the conventional and conservative look of many of the audience. We see the conservative nature of male fashion in the North East in the early 1960s represented in the image Down Beat Club in Worswick Street (*Figure 3*). The best known music club was the Club a Go Go in Newcastle's Percy Street which became legendary – particularly in relation to its role in promoting The Animals. It was also the key club venue in the city for performances by the major British Rock and Rhythm 'n' Blues performers of the period. Smaller clubs including La Cubana and The Bay Hotel in Sunderland and the New Cellar Club in South Shields also showcased major artistes and contributed as the decade progressed, to a night time culture for young people in which youth fashion played an increasingly significant part.

Newcastle of course, as I mentioned earlier, had its own sound which came from the Art College culture of the city. The Animals were never stylish and their uncompromising image matched the grittiness of their music and spoke of the sexual politics of the area. They had a predominantly male following and provided a contrast to the squeaky clean modernity of the early Beatles and the stylishness of the Small Faces. *We Gotta get Outa this Place* was recorded in 1964 and referred to the bleakness and remoteness of the Newcastle, and a culture in which the revolution in youth culture taking place in streets in London had a slow impact. Historically, there has been a strong differentiation in terms of gendered identity in the North East based on the traditional sexual division of labour and persisting even into the post-industrial present. Even by the mid-1960s, half a decade after the first mods were to be found in London, there were only a very small number of mods in Sunderland. The original mod identity was framed in the sophisticated milieu of the metropolis and had a Europeanised dimension, referring to Italian and French male fashion which brought a newly feminised quality to masculine style. Unisex grooming sat uncomfortably in the crude sexual politics of the North East until the mid-1960s. The few mods that there were in Sunderland, even by

1966, would gather in the Biz Bar near the bus station, a desultory group but representing something more exotic than the still persistent mainstream Reggie Trogg[7] identity that characterised many of the young men in the town and which was tied to traditional tropes of masculinity. There was a larger community of mods in Newcastle, many of whom would gather in the Haymarket area, near the University. However, the mod identity was still less influential in the North East than in provincial centres such as Wigan in the period. It wasn't until the mid to later 1960s – and Brian Ferry was performing with the group The Gas Board and "hippie culture" began to have an influence – that new more sophisticated masculinities were being widely represented on the city streets.

In examining the significance of the gender polarisation endemic in the region in contemporary culture in *Fashioning the Feminine* (Cheryl Buckley and Hilary Fawcett, 2002: 137), I recognised an exaggerated even camp identity in female fashioning. Some of this is explained perhaps by extreme gender stereotyping, but issues of class and cultural awareness are factors in local identities. There was an allegiance in some sites to role models such as Dusty Springfield or Susan Maugham, who were more glamorous in a 1950s sense and less metropolitan in their image than the ultra trendy Sandie Shaw or Julie Christie. Many young people even in the mid to late 1960s were tied to the region and had limited options financially. Freeman's Catalogue had a teenage range in the later 1960s which used Lulu as a model. In photographs of girls at the Mayfair or Mecca Ballroom we find bouffant hair "a la Lulu", white shiny Courreges inspired boots and abundant white crocheted dresses, which amounted to a set of 60s fashion clichés. In a short film from the BBC archives on fashion from Fenwicks in Newcastle in the mid-1960s we see a regional interpretation of op-art influenced fashion bordering on parody, which refers more to *Doctor Who* than John Bates or Andre Courreges.[8] Perhaps in this context cultural and geographical distance lent a distorting perspective to fashion and fashioning, an over-stylisation resulting from desperation to be seen to connect with metropolitan fashion values.

In a wider sense fashion and femininity were inscribed with societal and cultural tensions of enormous complexity. The idea that the mini skirt connoted some sudden freeing of sexual restraint for young women across Britain is a popular misconception. For every metropolitan sophisticate who apparently enjoyed new sexual freedoms there were many more young women from London itself, but also from different regional backgrounds and identities and for whom the period was wrought with contradictions and difficulties in negotiating a position for themselves within a changing cultural and social economy. Elizabeth Wilson in

Only Halfway to Paradise (Wilson, 1980) makes an analysis of the complexity of sexual politics and sexuality for women in the period, which illustrates that for all the apparent new confidence of young women evoked by the constant images of swinging chicks having a good time, the reality was much more problematic. The image of Twiggy with her anorexic looking body and highly revealing clothes represented the tensions which existed in a newly sexualised culture for women, at once powerless and enfranchised. Linda Grant in *Sexing the Millennium* (Grant, 1993: 205) claims that real sexual liberation didn't really happen until the early 1970s and in regional sites this was particularly true. For me and many of my peers, despite an increasingly provocative take on fashion, our appearance was at odds with our aspirations in which an engagement ring was just as significant as it had been for my mother's generation.

Anticipating a Fashion Revolution, 1967–71

On beginning my studies at Newcastle University in 1967, a rather naïve local girl, I was confronted by a perplexing and overwhelming world of post-Warhol cool. One of a minority of women on my degree, many of my fellow students came from London, having already done Art Foundation courses and were seemingly immersed in a decadent and sophisticated social milieu far removed from Sunderland's folk clubs. There was a distinct town and gown split with central Newcastle still dominated by a macho working class drinking culture and myself and fellow students spending our time in Jesmond and other areas outside the city. In cities across the country universities and art colleges represented arenas of stylish innovation, and as the decade wore on, counter cultural experimentation. I became more concerned with my appearance, dieting avidly and constantly pouring over copies of French *Elle* and *Vogue*. Image became an overriding preoccupation as I, like many of my peers, was consumed by the increasing media preoccupation with fashion. We would hitch-hike to London and buy clothes from Biba and Bus Stop, which seemed an extremely exciting alternative to that which was available in Newcastle. The metropolitan had taken over from the local, you had to travel to buy distinctiveness in the context of local culture, but in doing so some of the fun of customising and improvising which had been part of the experience of dislocation from major fashion markets was lost to the formulaic identity of dominant fashion.

However, Newcastle by the end of the 1960s had developed new retail identities in terms of women's fashion. In the Handyside Arcade near the University, small boutiques had opened including Kaleidoscope, Blaise, Target and Fig Leaf. They sold cheap and sometimes poorly made clothes, disposable and never quite matching the metropolitan ideal. The Arcade had an "alternative ambience", the smell of incense and patchouli oil hovering in the air in tribute to Haight-Ashbury. Elle Boutique which opened near the Handyside Arcade and the Club a Go Go in Percy Street was run by graduates of the Fashion School at Newcastle Art College. In 1963 a new qualification, the Diploma in Art and Design had been nationally established and the Fashion Department under the leadership of Mary Bromly, which was to develop one of the strongest provincial courses in fashion design in Britain. Elle Boutique stocked Ossie Clark, as well as their own designs and was very popular with the student population. In London initiatives such as Selfridges youth orientated retailing development Miss Selfridge, which opened in 1966 and the Way In in-store boutique in Harrods in 1967, had paved the way for the development of in-store boutiques in major regional department stores. Fenwicks had the most impressive of these in Newcastle in the later 1960s, but still couldn't compete with the metropolitan equivalent. Even smaller department stores in the region such as Parrishes on Shields Road or Joplings in Sunderland had their own versions of the in-store boutique, from which pop music blared out across the shop floor. The occasional more fashionable London-based initiative like the Sacha shoe shop in Grainger Street began to intimate some kind of changing retail profile, but it was a slow process.

Although outlets such as Top Man, City Stylish and even Butch Boutique in Percy Street sold a version of fashionable men's clothes, male fashion in Newcastle in the period was synonymous with Marcus Price. Marcus Price was a relatively up-market retailing identity selling stylish clothes which exuded a metropolitan cool and sophistication. With outlets in the Groat Market, Percy Street and later in Greys Street, he was the first retailer in the region to sell Levis and he also introduced key 1960s male fashion staples Ben Sherman shirts and Ravel shoes to Newcastle. He recalls shirts being the big fashion story for him in the 1960s with the Ben Sherman brand selling out as soon as he received a delivery. Although acknowledging that his shops weren't quite as on trend as those in London he did connect very strongly with a metropolitan identity and dressed the most fashion conscious men in the area including Bryan Ferry[9] (*see Figure 4*). There wasn't an equivalent women's fashion outlet in terms of style in Newcastle at this time. Obviously, women's fashion was more complex and multi directional, thus making it more difficult for provincial retailers to keep up with fast moving stylistic change.

Fashion provision for young people the city, particularly young women, was still limited at the end of the 1960s. Newcastle is the focus for a copy of *Honey* magazine in March 1969. All the young people interviewed even here on the edge of the 1970s claimed that there was still little that was interesting about fashion retailing in the city, or entertainment for young people and that London was still the Mecca to which everyone wished to escape. Photographs used to illustrate the editorial show models standing in a highly industrialised landscape wearing clothes sourced in London, as if to reinforce the notion of the North East as a fashion desert (*see Figure 5*). Of course that wasn't entirely true and there were increasing options for young people in terms of fashion retailing, however it wasn't until the early 1970s when fashion shops such as Bus Stop, Miss Selfridge and the home grown Victoria and Albert Boutique brought a version of the metropolitan 1960s to the North East. This marked the beginning of an increasing cultural homogeneity, in which regional difference becomes less significant in terms of fashion and fashioning.

Notes

1. Cilla Black was most famously dressed in clothes designed by John Bates, one of the major designers of the mid-1960s. Bates actually came from the North East originally but established his career in London, initially working as a window designer for Mary Quant and later designing women's clothes for several major manufacturers.

2. Mary Quant used a subtle palette of sludgy colours – maroons, mustards as well as the ubiquitous black. Her designs show an engagement with an Arts and Crafts inspired idea of good taste, despite their revolutionary nature in terms of style.

3. Richard Hoggart's *The Uses of Literacy* published in 1957 and Nancy Mitford's *Noblesse Oblige* (1956), both in their very different ways contributed to debates about class, culture and national identity.

4. Clothes rationing ended in 1952.

5. Karel Reiz directed *We are the Lambeth Boys* which was released in 1959.

6. John Crosby famously coined the term "Swinging London" in an article which he wrote for *Time Life* magazine in 1966. In it he was referring to the glamorous and sexy world of Jean Shrimpton, Julie Christie, Mick Jagger *et al.* which was centered around the Kings Road in Chelsea.

7. Reggie Trogg, lead singer of the Troggs, whose image was that of a bucolic teddy boy.

8. Short film from BBC Archive, Nation on Film, showing a fashion show in Fenwicks Newcastle in the mid-1960s.

9. Sting gives an account of dressing for a night at the Club a Go Go in 1966 in a Ben Sherman shirt and Levis in *Broken Music. A Memoir.*

Bibliography

Breward C., Gilbert, D. & Jenny Lister (eds) (2006) *The Swinging Sixties.* London: V and A Publications.

Barnes, R. (1979) *Mod!* London: Eel Pie Publishing Ltd.

Buckley, C. & Fawcett, H. (2002) *Fashioning the Feminine. Representation and Women's Fashion from the Fin de siecle to the Present.* London: I B Tauris.

Docherty, G. (2002) *A Promoters Tale. Rock at the Sharp End.* London, Omnibus.

Fogg, M. (2003) *Boutique. A 60s Cultural Phenomenon.* London: Mitchell Beazley.

Grant, L. (1993) *Sexing the Millennium. A Political History of the Sexual Revolution.* London: Harper Collins.

Green, J. (1999) *All Dressed Up. The Sixties and the Counterculture.* London: Pimlico.

Lancaster, B. (1995) *The Department Store. A Social History, London.* Leicester University Press, p.19.

McRobbie, A. (1980) *'Settling accounts with subcultures: a feminist critique'.* Screen International, 34.

Mort, F. (1997) in M. Nava, A. Blake, I. MacRury, & B. Richards (eds) *Buy This Book. Studies in Advertising and Consumption.* London: Routledge.

Sandbrook, D. (2005) *Never Had it so Good. A History of Britain from Suez to the Beatles. Britain in the Sixties 1956-63.* London: Little Brown.

Sinclair, N.T. (2004) *Sunderland. City and People since 1945.* Derby: Breedon Books.

Sting (2003) *Broken Music.* London: Pocket Books.

Wilson, E. (1980) *Only Halfway to Paradise: Women in Post War Britain: 1945-1968.* Tavistock.

Worth, R. (2007) *Fashion for the People. A History of Clothing at Marks and Spencer.* London: Berg.

Chapter Three

Changing Urban Landscapes: Architecture and Planning in Newcastle and Gateshead since 1945

Thomas Faulkner, Peter Beacock and Paul Jones

Perhaps unexpectedly, given their strategic and economic importance, the central areas of Newcastle and Gateshead survived the Second World War largely undamaged by bombing. However, the region soon suffered drastically in the post-war recession and, with a programme of mine closures beginning as early as the 1950s, the North East's reliance on traditional heavy industry began to change irrevocably in favour of the service sector.

Architecturally, the centre of Newcastle at this time still represented a coherent expression of Georgian and Victorian classicism, while Gateshead retained a significant legacy of Victorian and earlier housing. However, both conurbations were very run-down and faced serious problems of traffic congestion. Through traffic converged on the Tyne Bridge, with its bottle-neck to the north, while the main route from London to Edinburgh still passed along Newcastle's main shopping street (Northumberland Street).

The first radical attempt to solve problems of this kind was made in 1945 under the terms of Newcastle Corporation's new *Plan for Newcastle upon Tyne Report of the Town Planning Sub-Committee* and consisted of a proposal to build a ring road around the heart of the city. It would have run from the Tyne Bridge to the south of Brandling Place on its eastern side, and from the High Level Bridge to Queen Victoria Road via the Bigg Market and Newgate Street on its western. This was perhaps sensible enough but, even allowing for the obvious financial constraints of the period, it can be no surprise that most of the ideas contained within this Plan remained unexecuted. For example, its exaggeratedly modernist vision of a future city centre was closer to science fiction than practical urban planning. More credible, however, was its proposal to move the hub of the city northwards to Barras Bridge, in the vicinity of which a new Civic Centre, a substantial educational precinct, and a major new shopping centre (around Northumberland Street) were to be developed. Significantly, though, in view of the demolitions that were to come, this proposal would have destroyed a substantial part of the city's architectural heritage.

Before long, in response to the new Town and Country Planning Act of 1947, Newcastle Corporation produced in 1951 a second, broadly similar development plan. However, little was done until the 1960s, probably because of continuing post-war economic stringency and Newcastle's geographical remoteness. Now Wilfred Burns (1923–84) became the city's first specialist Chief Planning Officer and the local Labour politician T. Dan Smith (1915–93), who was later jailed for corruption, the Leader of the Council. Smith's slogan, "the Brasilia of the North" captured popular imagination, while also emphasising the fact that Newcastle's leaders were now prepared to sacrifice much of the city's essentially classical Georgian and Victorian heritage in their search for a new image based on International Modernism (*see Figure 1*).

The partnership between Smith and Burns produced the all-important 1963 Development Plan (Faulkner, 1996: 138–39). Its main concerns were traffic congestion, continuing economic decline and the perceived need for modernisation. It was much more radical than the 1945 and 1951 plans, even though substantially influenced by them. Another major difference was that many (although not all) elements of this newer plan were at last implemented, including, for example, one deriving from schemes proposed as early as the 1930s, the development of a major education precinct near the new Civic Centre. This formed the basis of what later became Newcastle Polytechnic and subsequently Northumbria University.

The 1963 Plan retained elements from earlier plans, including a new street aligned east of Northumberland Street (the present John Dobson Street). Similarly, its idea for an enlarged central motorway was based on the earlier concept of an inner eastern ring road. A new proposal, however, was that for a central motorway from the Redheugh Bridge to the Great North Road via the Haymarket, to be linked to the projected eastern motorway by two major east-west routes. One of these latter routes, from the New Bridge Street intersection to the Haymarket, would have actually passed underground – with the aim of separating traffic and pedestrian routes, as advocated by Le Corbusier. Indeed, such was the hero-worship of the veteran modernist architect and theorist at this time that T. Dan Smith even fantasised about employing him for the design of new buildings in Newcastle.

The 1963 Plan also contained important, if only partially realised proposals, for the regeneration of the quayside and the comprehensive redevelopment of both Eldon Square as a prestigious shopping complex, with a new hotel on its western side, and the area around New Bridge Street and John Dobson Street. The latter was to involve a new Central Library (*see Figure 2*) and Museum overlooked by a residential tower spanning the road.

Even Newcastle's unique Town Moor could not escape the attention of the planners at this time. This historic amenity of inalienable grazing land, to the north west of the city centre, had been saved from enclosure or urban development through its ownership by the Freemen of Newcastle and thanks to a specific Act of Parliament of 1774. Now, however, a Council Report of 1961 judged that much of it was in poor condition and not used to the city's best social and recreational advantage (*Proceedings of the Newcastle Council*, 1961: 4). In addition, it went on to suggest that the Moor should now contain playing fields and car parks, and its great expanses "be broken up and harmonised by more tree planting" (*Proceedings of the Newcastle Council*, 1961: 8).

A further report of 1965, commissioned from the designer Prof. Mischa Black, proposed the holding of a major Industrial Exhibition on the Moor and the subsequent permanent construction of roads, a sports stadium and multi-sports centre. Sufficient momentum was generated by these ideas for the Council to quickly organise a competition for a "Landscape Master Plan for the Town Moor", based on the above and seeking above all to create a series of more intimate areas, integrated together. Perhaps rather ominously, the professional journal *Northern Architect* did not approve. Apparently hinting at a preference for comprehensive redevelopment, it doubted "the viability of the entire notion of this enormous open space", proclaiming "can it really be justified other than in terms of sentiment or political inertia?" (*Northern Architect*, 1966: 650). In any event, of nineteen schemes submitted, the winner was that of Derek Lovejoy & Associates of Croydon, who, in a manner typical of the time, proposed that new roads across the Moor should be placed in cuttings, augmented by numerous bridges over the projected new motorway system (*Northern Architect*, 1966: 650). The assessors were pleased to note that "details such as over- and under-passes, levels and pedestrian ways are very fully worked out" (*Northern Architect*, 1966: 650). However, nothing came of this ambitious scheme.

Returning to the more general 1963 Development Plan, discussed earlier, it is worth noting that although this was well received at the time, it has subsequently had a very bad press. This was mainly because of such mistakes as its alignment of the central motorway (east) too close to the city centre and its over-eager, even enthusiastic demolition of Georgian, Victorian and other historic buildings. In this context the destruction of Eldon Square and the Royal Arcade, two major examples (1825–31 and 1831–32 respectively) of the celebrated early nineteenth-century collaboration between entrepreneur Richard Grainger and architect John Dobson, seemed to strike at the very heart of the city's identity (Faulkner, 1996: 141–44).

Hardly surprisingly therefore, the plan's more worthy (and unspectacular) proposals to conserve and improve the "Grainger-Dobson" central area of Grey,

Grainger and Clayton Streets (Burns, 1967: 32, 71–74), to create conservation areas, and to revitalise some areas of older housing elsewhere, are now largely forgotten. Similarly, its various failings were only further highlighted by the non-completion of some of its more important proposals. These included the scheme for a new cultural centre near New Bridge Street, where, incidentally, most of the new buildings that were constructed have been, or are about to be, demolished.

During this period a number of important, if unexecuted redevelopment proposals were also submitted by architects working in the private sector. Examples included Ryder & Yates's innovative Tyne Deck scheme of May 1969 which, remarkably, foreshadowed many of the ideas about linkage that ultimately led to the construction of the Gateshead Millennium Bridge, discussed later in this chapter. Presupposing the removal of the political boundary between Newcastle and Gateshead and the formation of a new, unitary city of Tyneside, the scheme had as its main feature a vast platform to be built across the Tyne. Lying between the Tyne Bridge and a point approximately half way towards the site of the present Gateshead Millennium Bridge, this would have contained major public buildings relating to the administration of this new city. It would also have incorporated a complete road system, sluice gates for the control of the river's water level, and, at its access points, multi-storey car parks (*Northern Architect*, 1969: 70–74).

Yet some of the elements even of this visionary project had been anticipated a few years before by a leader article in *Northern Architect* (probably by local architect Edward Nicklin) which had also called for the unification of Tyneside into a single city. For this, it proposed a centre actually spanning the Tyne. "Archigram"-style accompanying drawings (by Derek Lawson) showed a monumental bridge, sited between the Tyne Bridge and the Swing Bridge and housing a superstructure containing shops, restaurants, offices and night clubs, as well as a hotel, theatre, dance hall and bowling alley (*Northern Architect*, 1965: 564–65).

In Newcastle, noteworthy post-war buildings that were actually constructed include Swan House, in Pilgrim Street, designed by Sir Robert Matthew and Partners (1963–69). This former office complex, occupying a roundabout at a motorway intersection, was an integral part of the city's redevelopment plan, and constituted one of the major "gateways" to what T. Dan Smith called the "modern city wall" of the new central motorway (east) (Smith, 1970: 51). However, Swan House only served to block the northern exit of the Tyne Bridge from its natural outlet into Pilgrim Street and, equally controversially, was built on the very site of Grainger and Dobson's much-admired Royal Arcade. Yet the structure itself is far from being a monolithic and oppressive block. It has clean modernist lines, and – before its recent partial demolition during a process of conversion into luxury apartments – successfully integrated an ingenious variety of contrasting textures, levels and forms.

The slightly later MEA House, in Ellison Place, was completed in 1974. This striking building was the first purpose-built centre for voluntary charitable organisations in the country. In response to the constraints of the site, its floors and pedestrian decks are suspended, by means of ties connected to four main girders at roof level, while its rectilinear main block is clad in mirror glass. Overall, the uncompromising modernism of its forms, relating rather incongruously to the early nineteenth-century town houses nearby, is highly characteristic of the work of its designers, Gordon Ryder and Peter Yates. Their celebrated practice of Ryder & Yates (now Ryder HKS), mentioned earlier, was originally founded in the early 1950s, after its principals had first met when they both joined the Peterlee (New Town) Development Corporation in 1948.

An attractive miniature from a decade or so earlier is the Denton Branch Library on West Road, dating from 1960–61. It has the appearance of a white, modernist pavilion, its north elevation being almost entirely glazed. Its architect, Harry Wood, was one of several distinguished practitioners then working at the Newcastle University of Architecture. His low-cost, non-traditional design, involving a large, uninterrupted internal space, reflected his careful analysis of the environmental factors affecting a building of this kind.

At the other end of the scale is the Newcastle Civic Centre, on Barras Bridge (*see Figure 3*). Construction began in 1958 and continued in stages for another ten years, although design work – by the then City Architect, George Kenyon – had begun as early as 1950. Not surprisingly, the building, although unique in Britain, was regarded as decidedly old-fashioned when finally complete. Its design was intended to be a departure from tradition, with no monumental facade or grand entrance. Instead, the emphasis is on the expressive articulation of a number of distinct elements. These include the Rates Hall (the east block), an adjoining twelve-storey administrative range to the north, the Carillon Tower to the west, the adjacent Council Chamber, which, incidentally, is cylindrical in form, and the Banqueting Hall just to the north of this. Moreover, the Centre's general accessibility is highlighted by the provision of entrances from a number of approaches.

Yet the building is as lavish as any traditional civic hall, and seems in many ways to typify the early post-war desire for richness and sparkle following the success of

Figure 1: Below: Artist's impression of a modernised and redeveloped Northumberland Street, Newcastle, c.1963 (image from the Archive of Napper Architects Ltd, original architects: Alec Collerton, Bill Barnett, Chris Rainford, Bill Hall, Eric Carter).

Figure 2: Above: The former Central Library, Princess Square, Newcastle, by Sir Basil Spence & Partners, 1966–68 (now demolished): from the north west. Photograph: Tom Yellowley.

Figure 3: Right: The Civic Centre, Barras Bridge, Newcastle, by George Kenyon, 1958–68: the Council Chamber and west side of tower. Photograph: Tom Yellowley.

Figure 4: Left: The Baltic Centre for Contemporary Art, South Shore Road, Gateshead, converted by Dominic Williams (Ellis Williams), 1994–2002: from the west. Photograph: Tom Yellowley.

Figure 5: Below: The Gateshead Millennium Bridge, Newcastle-Gateshead quayside, by Wilkinson Eyre with Gifford & Partners, 1996–2001: from the north east; in the background, the Sage Gateshead music centre, by Foster & Partners, 1997–2004. Photograph: Tom Yellowley.

Figure 6: Above Right: 'i6 Charlotte Square', Newcastle (conversion by Bill Hopper Design, 2004): from the south west. Photograph: Tom Yellowley.

the Festival of Britain in 1951. Thus there are unusually costly facing materials, such as marble, and rich, even exotic, wood veneers internally, and varying forms of Portland stone and Norwegian Otta slate externally. All these combine to give distinctly Scandinavian overtones. Also, as at Coventry Cathedral, another major building of the period, the Centre expensively incorporates the work of numerous artists, designers and craftsmen, in this case including Geoffrey Clarke, John Hutton, J.R.M. McCheyne, Victor Pasmore, John Piper, Charles Sansbury, A.B. Reid and David Wynne.

Elsewhere, some of the city's most significant post-war buildings are those commissioned by Newcastle University, an institution that tried hard to maintain the overall quality of its developments. A good example is the Stephenson Building, on Claremont Road. This was one of the first structures to be built in accordance with the University's post-war master plan, as drawn up by Prof. W.B. Edwards, then Head of the School of Architecture, and Sir Howard Robertson. Designed by Edwards himself in 1951–52, the building is characterised by block-like forms and is faced in plain, buff brick. With its long, four-storey principal facade, it is a restrained, still fairly conservative design not untypical of the very early post-war years.

More unequivocally modernist is the slightly later Herschel (Physics) Building, on the Haymarket (by Sir Basil Spence and Partners, 1957–62), an eight-storey horizontal block having panels of dark grey slate placed between metal windows. So too are the buildings lying slightly nearer to Barras Bridge and bounded by King's Walk, Claremont Road and Queen Victoria Road. These form an important group comprising the six-storey Daysh Building, the twelve-storey Claremont Tower and Merz Court, a six-storey, semi-enclosed block with an open, trapezium-shaped courtyard in the centre. Constructed in 1964–68 to the designs of Richard Sheppard, Robson and Partners, this complex formed the centrepiece of the University's major expansion programme after it achieved independent status from Durham in 1963. Its use of ribbon windows throughout reveals the more overt use of a concrete frame structure, although once again the buildings are faced predominantly in brick.

The exception occurs where the Daysh Building (for Geography) links to a major extension to the Department of Fine Art, along King's Walk. This extension, built of exposed concrete, is a powerful horizontal form, unashamedly influenced by the later work of Le Corbusier. Much the same architectural language is also used in Sir William Whitfield's nearby extension to the Students' Union (1961–63), in which large windows, protected by a complex "brise-soleil" of pre-cast concrete, create a highly articulated facade.

Meanwhile, in the rather more workaday environment south of the Tyne, the Great North Road was being re-aligned in the early 1960s to provide a dual carriageway by-passing the centre of Gateshead. The town itself also saw massive redevelopment, mainly to provide new shopping facilities. The main result of this was the construction between 1964 and 1969 of the enormous and always controversial Trinity Square shopping centre and multi-storey car park, designed by the Owen Luder Partnership. This concrete "megastructure" now dominates the Gateshead skyline.

Otherwise, curiously, the town possesses little significant architecture from the earlier post-war period. However, its own Borough Architect's Department produced a certain amount of competent work, for example the high-rise flats either side of the A1 to the south of the town centre, or the former Dryden Road Grammar School for Girls, opened in 1956, while the private sector was responsible for the dramatic Felling Pool, at the Leam Lane estate (by Napper, Errington & Collerton, 1961–63).

Throughout Tyneside this was a period of widespread "slum clearance", with older dwellings being replaced by then-fashionable medium- and high-rise, system-built housing. Ironically, many of these modernist blocks have now been demolished. Yet one entirely different type of housing development that did emerge can be found at Newcastle's "Byker Wall" estate (mainly by the Swedish-based English architect Ralph Erskine, c.1969–81). The approach here involved a more informal style of architecture, with much use of wood and brick, and was based on consultation, linked to a system of progressive re-housing to retain community cohesion. Also unusual for the period – and prophetic of "post-modern" developments to come – was the building's incorporation of symbolic references, as for example that to the idea of a protective wall. This resonates powerfully in Newcastle, given the historic legacy of both Hadrian's Wall (which passed nearby) and the medieval Town Wall.

Turning to the more contemporary period from c.1975 to the present day, we find that now, as elsewhere, the architecture of Newcastle and Gateshead can no longer be categorised by any particular style, type, or approach. However, much of it can be described as "post-modern"; sometimes it even displays a tendency towards pastiche. This contrasts markedly with the area's earlier firm commitment to modernism. Nor was any such perceived inconsistency helped by the numerous economic recessions during these years.

However, the period ended strongly, with major programmes of urban renewal along both sides of the Tyne. Various redevelopment schemes had been proposed, before Gateshead Council, very creditably, took the initiative by planning major new quayside art and music centres, with a new pedestrian bridge connecting these facilities to the Newcastle side. For a time, its capital works programme actually overshadowed schemes planned by its larger neighbour to the north, and the Baltic Art Centre (*see Figure 4*), the Gateshead Millennium Bridge and the Sage Gateshead music centre (*see Figure 5*) have brought fame and recognition to a hitherto unglamorous area. Meanwhile, in partnership with the Tyne and Wear Development Corporation, Newcastle Council also became active in redeveloping its quayside, around the earlier new Law Courts (mentioned below). From 1991 it employed Newcastle University graduate Sir Terry Farrell to produce a master plan for the area. All these developments will be discussed in more detail later in this chapter.

In terms of individual buildings, "post-modernism" began to feature strongly during the first half of the 1980s, even though this period was in many ways a depressing one for the region, with further industrial decline and high unemployment. The dramatic and colourful Elswick Swimming Pool, off Elswick Road, Newcastle, was built in 1979–81 to the designs of the Napper Collerton Partnership. Lying on the site of the former Elswick Hall (demolished in 1978), it utilises corrugated metal cladding and full-height, mirrored glazing, while the roof structure projects out to form a canopy running the full length of the pool on the south side. The pool itself is an amorphous shape that contrasts sharply with the rectilinear structure of the building as a whole. Even more overtly "post-modern" are the Law Courts, on Newcastle's quayside, built in 1984–90 to the designs of the same architects. Here they adopted an updated, eclectic version of the neo-classical style, the facade of the building that faces the river having gigantic Tuscan columns. Clad in eye-catching red sandstone, this facade also features porthole windows, perhaps referencing Newcastle's maritime heritage.

Among other practitioners operating in Newcastle, Jane and David Darbyshire (now active as the separate practices of JDDK and Darbyshire Architects) deserve mention for some sensitive yet innovative work, mainly in a more neo-vernacular style. This includes the St Oswald's Hospice, in Regent Avenue, Newcastle (completed 1987), a largely single-storey building that evokes the image of a medieval almshouse. Its use of natural materials such as brick, tile and especially timber, also suggests a neo-Arts and Crafts approach. Much the same can be said of Jacobin's Court, in Stowell Street, Newcastle, designed by Jane Darbyshire alone. This is a small mixed-use development, of 1991–92, that is carefully related to the adjacent historic fabric of Blackfriars cloister.

An important recent building in Newcastle is the International Centre for Life, on Forth Banks (1996), designed by Sir Terry Farrell and Partners. This is a national facility for exploring genetic science and was also intended to provide a new western "gateway" into the city. Its architecture is complicated, combining both organic and rectilinear forms. The most striking element of the overall complex is "Life Interactive World", a visitor attraction comprising an exhibition space with an educational facility. It comprises a "black box" structure of metal, with glazed screen walls, that contrasts dramatically with its entrance; the latter has an unusual, amorphous shape, resembling that of a folded leaf.

Also in recent years there has been a progressive movement of population back into the urban centres, where, interestingly, the finest new developments have tended to be renovations or conversions of existing structures. Local architects such as Bill Hopper have made a mark with the fashionable new apartments created within the Victorian former Turnbull's Warehouse on the Newcastle quayside. Hopper was also responsible for the imaginative conversion into offices of the former warehouse at No. 85 City Road, Newcastle, in 2000. Here he maintained many of the warehouse's original features, exposing its heavy steel frame and roof trusses, while also using coloured render to achieve a striking external effect.

Yet another example of his work can be seen at "i6 Charlotte Square", Newcastle, an ingenious conversion and amalgamation (2004) of two adjoining properties in this historic square, a three-storey, eighteenth-century house, and a four-storey warehouse dating from the 1930s (*see Figure 6*). The principal feature of this scheme is a glazed atrium that links and lights these two original buildings, its sharp lines contrasting effectively with their brick surfaces as well as with the weathered stone of the adjacent medieval Town Wall.

Within the expanding education sector, Newcastle University has continued to enlarge its campus. More recently it has shown admirable commitment to energy-conscious architecture, as with the Devonshire Building, off Claremont Road, a new environmental research facility opened in 2004 (architects: the Dewjoc

Partnership). It contains six storeys of laboratories and open-plan offices, and incorporates numerous energy-efficient features such as photovoltaic panels, passive ventilation and a "grey water" recycling system. Internally, a large atrium admits large amounts of natural light, while the building's exterior effectively references "high-tech" design of the 1970s and 80s.

Meanwhile, Northumbria University has been responsible for the sensitive renovation of some of its nineteenth-century building stock, including houses in Ellison Place, Newcastle, and the nearby Sutherland Building and Burt Hall. It is also presently creating a new campus on the former Warner Brothers Cinema site on the eastern side of the central motorway. Nor have innovative developments been confined to the University sector. West of Newcastle's city centre is the new (2004) Performance Academy of Newcastle College, on the Rye Hill Campus at Scotswood Road. This eye-catching structure, by architects RMJM, is one of the largest single educational facilities for music, performance, arts and media in the country. Its fully-glazed ground floor contrasts dramatically with the entrance, executed in concrete and serving as a foyer to the theatre element of the design.

The variety and importance of the later post-war buildings discussed above is undeniable. Even so, by far the most significant contribution to the changing urban landscape of Newcastle and Gateshead during this period has been that made by the spectacular redevelopment of the formerly near-derelict quaysides along both banks of the Tyne. Here, although the potential for redevelopment had been recognised as early as the 1960s, little or nothing was done for more than twenty years. Then, in 1987, the newly-formed Tyne and Wear Development Corporation identified the regeneration of Newcastle's east quayside as a potential flagship scheme. In 1991, as mentioned earlier, a master plan for the redevelopment of the area was commissioned from architects Sir Terry Farrell and Partners, providing design guidelines and a framework for development.

Farrell's plan prioritised the pedestrian, who, he felt, had tended to be neglected in more orthodox, "reactive" schemes. His aim was, in his own words, "the rediscovery of the quayside as a place" (Farrell *et al.*, 2002: 208), utilising an innovative layout that is "like the beads of a necklace" to achieve "a seamless integration between the existing context and new interventions" (Farrell *et al.*, 2002: 210–12). Buildings were therefore arranged to resemble warehouses, with the spaces between them reflecting the narrow lanes between old structures of this kind (Farrell *et al.*, 2002: 210).

The successful implementation of this plan totally transformed the old quayside, which now possesses an exciting mix of buildings, mainly for commercial, residential and leisure purposes. A good example is the "Pitcher and Piano" public house, completed in 1997 to the designs of architects Panter Hudspith. This is constructed predominantly of ashlar sandstone and, on three sides, of glass. Magnificent views are created, both outward along the river, and inward to the large and lofty bar area. The roof, following a gentle, wave-like curve cleverly suggestive of a maritime environment, extends to form a deep canopy over the longest, glazed wall. Here a design standard was set for the whole east quayside, an area which was further enhanced by the addition of open squares, high-quality hard landscaping, and public works of art.

Yet despite this success, the newly-created views of the Tyne from Newcastle's quayside were initially marred by scenes of decay on the other side of the river. However, Gateshead Council's ambitious plans for the redevelopment of its own side of the river, including "Gateshead Quays", a formerly derelict stretch downstream of the Tyne Bridge (still ongoing), soon led to the construction of two major buildings for the arts. The Baltic Centre for Contemporary Art (by Dominic Williams of architects Ellis Williams, 1998–2002) and the Sage Gateshead music centre (by Foster and Partners, 1997–2004) are more spectacular than anything on the Newcastle side of the river and have achieved international renown.

Yet both would have remained comparatively isolated but for the presence of the Gateshead Millennium Bridge (by architects Wilkinson Eyre with engineers Gifford and Partners). The Millennium Bridge has succeeded in linking both sides of the river as never before. It has also served to create an attractive pedestrian circuit embracing both banks of the Tyne. Completed in 2001, this is the world's first tilting bridge and consists of a curved steel arch, with a laterally-curved walkway suspended from it by cables. When open, its two matching curves form the unique opening "eye", or "gateway". The bridge's lightness and elegance contrast markedly with the heavy engineering structure of the nearby Tyne Bridge (of 1924–28) and, like much of the quayside redevelopment generally, seems to symbolise Tyneside's evolution into a "post-industrial" phase, with its new, more leisure-based economy.

The Baltic goes even further in being an actual conversion of a redundant former industrial structure, namely the surviving silo element of the former Baltic Flour Mill, originally opened in 1950. The Baltic exemplifies a new type of highly flexible public art venue, an "art factory" rather than a gallery and comprises the redeveloped mill structure itself and a new "riverside" extension that provides the building's main entrance. Of the original massive mill building, only the longer north and south facades have been retained. The other walls have been replaced with glass, thus affording splendid views of the cityscape along the Tyne.

More controversial, though undeniably eye-catching, is the Sage Gateshead music centre, which lies slightly to the west of the Baltic, near the Tyne Bridge. Its amorphous, shell-like external form, of glistening stainless steel and glass, has been perceived as alien, and the building fails to achieve a fully-integrated relationship with the riverside, even though a glazed walkway in front of the three auditoria contained within it does form a valuable part of an open-access pedestrian route along the Tyne. As a music venue, however, it is world-class, employing the most up-to-date acoustic technology, and is popular with concert-goers and tourists alike.

With its innovative buildings, public spaces and walks, all for the first time effectively linked, the Newcastle and Gateshead quayside redevelopment has at last succeeded in exploiting the remarkable natural advantages of its site. And although much remains to be done, especially in terms of connecting the quayside to the main urban centres nearby, the riverside area itself has once again become busy and populated. More than fifty years ago the historian Nikolaus Pevsner famously described historic Durham as comparable architecturally only to Avignon and Prague (Pevsner, 1953: 77). Now, thanks to the redevelopment described above, Tyneside can also boast an urban landscape of European quality.

Bibliography

Burns, W. (1967) *Newcastle: a Study in Replanning at Newcastle upon Tyne*. London: Leonard Hill.

Farrell, T., Pearman, H. & Tobin, J. (2002) *Ten Years, Ten Cities: the Work of Terry Farrell and Partners, 1991-2001*. London: Laurence King Publishing.

Faulkner, T.E. (ed.) (1996) *Northumbrian Panorama: Studies in the History and Culture of North East England*. London: Octavian Press Ltd.

Northern Architect, September 1965, March 1966, May 1969.

Pevsner, N. (1953) *The Buildings of England: County Durham*. Harmondsworth: Penguin Books.

Proceedings of the Newcastle Council, "Town Moor and Parks Committee: Joint Report by the City Engineer, the City Estate and Property Surveyor, the Director of Parks and Cemeteries and the City Planning Officer", September 1961.

Smith, T.D. (1970) *Dan Smith: An Autobiography*. Newcastle upon Tyne: Oriel Press.

Chapter Four

Art and Design Education
in Post-war Newcastle

Shelagh Wilson

This chapter discusses the contribution of Art Schools as a key factor in the creation of the flourishing art culture of today's North East. The region has an extraordinary legacy of art school education, in both quality and quantity. No other city the size of Newcastle has two internationally recognised Higher Education institutions. There are also nearby universities such as Sunderland and a number of high quality colleges teaching art and design courses. Here the focus is on Newcastle and Northumbria Universities. But any consideration of the Northern "art world", must acknowledge the intermeshing links of education, exhibition, dialogue and audience that all the colleges contribute towards.

The often mutually antagonistic development of Fine Art and Design at Newcastle and Northumbria Universities had a tremendous influence on visual culture in the immediate post-war period. Newcastle University introduced the then new "preliminary course" based on the pioneering programme of the German Bauhaus, while Northumbria developed flagship design courses, which were amongst the first in the country to achieve validation. This post-war phase undoubtedly gave great opportunities for many young people in the North East to become some of the country's leading artists and designers. The oft-repeated pattern of this phase from the 1950s–70s was that to achieve success, one had to leave the North East, usually for good. The next phase, the one that is still ongoing, is the beginning of a move towards a "critical mass" of graduates from the universities *staying* in the North East – retaining a base there, or returning. There is now a core of exhibition spaces, studios, and most importantly, an audience for art. This is paralleled by a similar rise in activity in the performance arts, epitomized by the opening of the imposing Sage Gateshead centre. But while almost all commentators discussing the Sage Gateshead realise that the pioneering work of regional groups such as Northern Sinfonia and Folkworks were essential in building the audience to fill those vast auditoria, few credit achievement of the same "critical mass" in the visual arts to local educational institutions. However, I will argue that it is difficult to see how the Baltic could have flourished without them.

Golden Age

Although both the precursor colleges to Northumbria and Newcastle Universities existed before the Second World War, it is the post-war developments that concern us here.[1] The creation of modern art education followed the appointment of Lawrence Gowing as Professor of Fine Art in 1949, at what is now known as Newcastle University. The department, though physically present in Newcastle, was part of "King's College, University of Durham". Gowing's predecessor at Newcastle, Robin Darwin had found the work of students in 1948 to be "curiously, depressing – tired and dull ...and lacking in personal conviction" (Frayling, 1987: 131). Darwin left to become principal of the Royal College of Art, where he undertook a series of reforms which took it out of direct government control and towards University status as the only purely postgraduate Art College in Britain.

The Fine Arts represented at Newcastle were mainly painting and sculpture, but it also retained some teaching that was a residue of earlier courses with a strong Arts and Crafts bias. These fed into two preliminary courses taken by Fine Art students, one of which looked at the principles of deign and the other at fine art. Gowing appointed two very different artists to work with him. Victor Pasmore, appointed to teach the art component, had been a colleague from the Euston Road School. Pasmore would become known for his gently undulating pure abstractions, one of which now soothes visitors to Newcastle Civic Centre's social security offices. Richard Hamilton, appointed to teach design, was a very different figure. Now known as one of the founders of Pop Art, he became an avowed political radical. But both were united by the fact that they were then experimenting with a totally new approach to art education. They had both previously worked on experimental teaching at Camberwell, work which Pasmore had further developed with likeminded innovators[1] (*see Figure 1*).

In 1954 Pasmore brought his version of a basic course for fine art, which added to the work Hamilton was already pioneering for the same students on the design course. Hamilton later explained in an interview that, "the first aim of our course is a clearing of the slate; removing preconceptions" (Hamilton, 1966: 132). This was a beloved mantra of the modernist creed, the shared method of those who sought to introduce teaching of art and design based on "Bauhaus" principles. These had been developed on the "foundation course" of the Bauhaus in Germany, which had been established from 1919 by Johannes Itten, Paul Klee, Lazlo Moholy-Nagy and others.[2] The idea was to empty the mind: to create a *tabula rasa*, or razed ground on which fundamental principles of design could be built. John A. Walker, a Newcastle student from 1956–61 later recalled:

What also made the Department one of the most advanced and progressive in the country was the basic design course – referred to then as 'basic form' or the 'foundation course' – that was taught to first year students in groups and in blocks of time. Students were set exercises addressing the fundamentals of all art and design, that is, point, line, shape, colour, tone, texture, form, structure and space. (Walker, 2003: 12) [3]

Traditional art education, still taught and examined centrally to ensure conformity at most British Art schools, emphasized copying and drawing from pre-selected exemplars, with an emphasis on training of hand skills. This technique dated back to the founding of the government schools of design, which were centrally organised by Henry Cole in the mid-nineteenth century (Macdonald, 1970).

As an autonomous University degree, free from the heavy hand of central government control, the Fine Art staff at Newcastle University had considerable freedom in determining the approach and content of their teaching. Their analytical approach encouraged experimentation and initially led to abstract, simple and basic work in two and three dimensions. This is clear in Hamilton's and Pasmore's own work at this time. Pasmore, involved in the English Constructionist group, was producing reliefs from industrial materials, drawing on scientific theories of proportion, but still stressing aesthetic qualities. With him students engaged with basic forms in a series of "laboratory experiments". Hamilton was preoccupied with non-figurative art and strongly influenced by D'Arcy Thompson's "Growth and Form". These were combined with his growing interest in photography, film and American mass culture. There was a brief attempt to teach a shared single basic course in 1959–60. However the Bauhaus ideal of the "basic course" as a form of teaching common to Fine Art and Design was not fully executed. Whether the students fully benefited from the "revolution" they were subject to is hard to judge. Walker had his doubts:

...the basic design course exercises were disconnected for the most part from industrial design and architecture (although Pasmore himself was involved in architecture and Hamilton was involved with graphic and industrial design), and took place in a socio-political vacuum. At Newcastle, the only logical outcome of basic design course exercises for the fine art students appeared to be abstract paintings and constructions... However, their formal and analytical character did encourage abstraction. Students were taught to analyse and explore the elements of art and design but little or no advice was given concerning their re-combination or synthesis; the issue of content was also neglected even though Hamilton's first pop paintings were rich in subject matter. (Walker, 2003: 11) [4]

In her assessment Marion Scott points to the involvement with community and the "open minded approach and personal development of each student", as major benefits (Scott, 1996: 39). Pasmore's involvement with the New Town development at Peterlee is well known. Hamilton's design work at the Gulbekian Art Gallery at the Peoples's Theatre and the logo for Granada television perhaps less so. Certainly many graduates went on to establish major careers as artists: Ian Stephenson, Mark Lancaster, Rita Donagh, Tim Head, and Sean Scully for instance (and many others in other fields). However, for the history of art education it was the publicity and the influence the course had on the Coldstream Report which made it so significant.

The reputation of the Newcastle course became known through magazine articles and the series of exhibitions which publicized the work nationally. Hamilton, often in collaboration with Pasmore, created several influential shows at the Hatton Gallery, Newcastle. These were then transferred to London's ICA. Man, Machine and Motion (1955) was a reflection of Hamilton's concerns with seeking forms for basic design and his interest in images drawn from popular culture. "an EXHIBIT" (1957), with Pasmore, was "conceived as a game in which the final form of the work would be the result of "constructive improvisation, terminated arbitrarily on the planned opening date" (Thistlewood, 1981: 36). This early piece of installation and performance art prefigured the international lead Newcastle took in this field in the 1970s.

However, it was the exhibition "Developing Process" (1959) which most effectively advertised the new approaches developed by Pasmore and Hamilton. The title is explained by Pasmore's belief that:

> *The production of art is a developing process which originates in the first dimension, the making of a single point. By an expansion into the second dimension, drawing and painting, and into the third, sculpture or architecture, it is possible to achieve a developmental association between, at one extreme, the simple mark and, at the other, free-standing construction in space. (Thistlewood, 1981: 8)*

The exhibition reversed the usual trend, by being developed in Newcastle, then taken to London before touring the country. Not only was it seen by large numbers of art teachers and students but the timing coincided with deliberations that would result in "a radical transformation" of art education. The idea that fine art and design education should be linked together and should feed each other informed the deliberations of the National Advisory Council on Art Education. Pasmore also sat on the key committee (Strand, 1987: 8). Thus the ideas of Hamilton, Pasmore and other innovators (*see Figure 1*):

... had direct and indirect representation to the Coldstream Commission, and through its recommendation preparatory courses came into existence in every significant Art School and College in the country. Having to define course structures at quite short notice, many teachers were to refer, consciously or otherwise, to the ready prototype. (Thistlewood, 1981: 10)

The 4-year degree at Newcastle began with the preliminary basic course, but also included a compulsory component of Art history. This aspect was rooted in ideas of a liberal education, where analytical and critical enquiry and creative experimentation were encouraged. It was an influential model on the series of reports that revolutionized British Design Education in the 1960s. The first *Coldstream Report* recommended a new Diploma Course equivalent to a three year degree, preceded by pre-diploma preparation. This led to the widespread adoption of "foundation courses" in the manner pioneered at Newcastle. The new Diplomas were conceived as a "liberal education in art", closer in line to University humanities courses than the vocational and occupational training that Art Schools were providing. Perhaps the most radical and most attractive element of the first *Coldstream Report* was the recommendation to terminate centrally examined courses (the NDD). The new Diploma (Dip AD) would only be offered by those few colleges that could achieve the higher standard. The National Council for Diplomas in Art and Design (NCDAD, 1961) inspected all the colleges. The main requirements were quality of faculties, inclusion of a fine art base, staff and the ability to offer the required complementary and art historical studies. Standards were high. Of the 210 courses from sixty-one colleges that applied, only sixty-one courses at twenty-nine colleges were approved, leaving many colleges with no approved Diplomas (Macdonald, 1970: 355).

Many colleges gradually gained approval to validate their courses as they achieved the required standard. As Coldstream had intended, colleges who failed to gain approval for Dip AD had to diversify into full- and part-time vocational and leisure education. The process of separation of the "thinking and expressive" from the technical and practical student was further emphasized when the NCDAD merged with the Council for National Academic Awards (CNAA) in 1974. The CNAA, the validation body for the new Polytechnics, gradually revalidated many Dip Ads as the now familiar degree courses. However, the price for the development of tertiary art education in Newcastle, as elsewhere was the loss of foundation, BTec, HND and any other advanced work to the local Newcastle College if Art colleges were to become part of the New Polytechnics.

Figure 1: Left: Victor Pasmore (right).
Photograph: Newcastle University.

Figure 2: Below: Commercial Art ,Clayton Rd, 1955.
Photograph: Northumbria University.

Figure 3: Bottom: Display, Clayton Rd, 1955.
Photograph: Northumbria University.

JOURNAL 16/3/72

Peter Anthony

Fenwick chips away at his second saint

DO I detect, somewhere, a mounting enthusiasm for the Festival of Bede?

There seem to be several festivals for 1973-74 to mark the 1,300th anniversary of the birth of the Venerable Bede, who lived at Jarrow and was connected with Monkwearmouth.

But, so far as I can discover, there is only one Geordie sculptor who has ever sculptured figures of Bede. He was at work before the current festival was so much as a sparkle in the eye of the Bishop of Durham, or in the minds of other ministers who are now so interested.

Mr. Fenwick Lawson, 39-year-old head of the sculp-

ture department of Newcastle Polytechnic, and son of a Geordie miner from Craghead, first turned to sculpting Bede when he was a student at the Royal College of Art, London.

"My interest in St. Bede was because he was a Geordie saint," Mr. Lawson told me. "I wanted to identify my work with a Geordie saint."

Now Mr. Lawson has completed a more formal study of Bede, hewn out of elm, which presents the great scholar as a devotional figure.

Another sculpture is now taking shape, also being hewn out of elm.

"This Bede will be more monumental in the public sense," said Mr. Lawson. "He will be holding a quill

as a gesture that his work was inspired by God."

Now ministers of North-East churches are calling at Mr. Lawson's Polytechnic studio to admire his fine work. These, the work of a genuine Geordie artist, should have a place in any Bede festival.

"That a Bede festival is happening gives me a chance in a lifetime to make a meaningful statement through sculpture," Mr. Lawson said.

Geordie sculptor, Geordie saint: Fenwick Lawson with his Bede.

Figure 4: Above: Fenwick Lawson, Fine Art at Newcastle Polytechnic. Photograph: Northumbria University.

Figure 5: Below: Art Students, Newcastle Journal, 1971. Photograph: Northumbria University.

THE JOURNAL Wednesday March 3 1971

Three little maids from school

JOURNAL FASHION:

Anne Hughes

SUE BRYANT, Val Linley and Yvonne Goldfingle are three girls for whom clothes are a way of life.

As design students at Newcastle Polytechnic's School of Fashion, they are kept busy learning the finer points of the rag trade.

And naturally enough, these three little maids from school have very definite ideas about fashion.

"Fashion is fun," said Sue "I love clothes. At the moment you can wear any length you like, mini, midi, maxi, anything is OK."

"Yes," said Yvonne, "but I think that people are a bit confused by this and they end up not knowing what to wear."

On one thing they are all agreed. To dress well you need money.

"I don't have enough money to dress as I would like," said Sue. "My grant won't stretch that far, so I make a lot of my clothes myself.

"My mother has lots of old patterns from the 30's and 40's and I find these great for ideas. She even has the occasional piece of old material and these can look really unusual because they are so different from today's fabrics."

But if they did have the money, the girls wouldn't spend it in Newcastle.

"The shops here are hopeless," was Val's opinion.

"To get really good clothes you have to go to London. Even for fabrics, the ones I like are the pretty prints and you can't get them here."

THIS is Yvonne wearing a midi dress she designed and made herself. It's in grey bonded jersey with split skirt and V-neckline. The bold design is appliqued in black and silver-grey panne velvet.

Another fashion note is the feather choker. These are made and sold by another girl, Liz Jackson, who among other places finds the feathers in London's Portobello Road.

NEXT a design of Val's—a man's jump suit in black velour which can be worn with or without a see-through voile shirt. This was Val's answer to a question set in class. If the present custom was reversed and girls were expected to ask men for dates, what should men wear to be their most attractive? "I designed the suit like this to show off as many erogenous zones as possible," said Val.

THE pretty flowers and elves motif is also an idea of Val's—this time for a fabric design. Sparked off by an interest in children's book illustrations, it's meant for printing on voile or silk.

THE leggy dolly is a sketch by Sue of an outfit she has made for herself. The blouse was actually made in black crepe and adapted from a 1939 pattern. The bodice is gathered in pin tucks from the shoulder seam. With it are dark brown velvet shorts made from a trouser pattern.

LAST lady in line shows an ambitious fabric design of Sue's for a coat. Since it's unique it's already well known as her "castle coat." The pattern in shades of pink and maroon is to be carefully screen printed on canvas.

The Fine Art Degree at Newcastle was not only exceptional for its pioneering role in art education. It was also the exception for the majority of young people who aspired to be practicing artists and designers. It took a small elite of well qualified students. In the immediate post-war period very few, especially those with working class origins, were able to attend university. In addition, despite a small amount of "textile printing and stained glass", the university course was, as now, largely restricted to Fine Art: painting and sculpture. Aspiring practical designers had to look elsewhere. Aspirant designers such as local girl Wendy Ramshaw, like the majority of students, were reliant on the government system of art education run by colleges such as Sunderland Art School and the art and design courses at Rutherford College (now part of Northumbria University. The realization of the need for such education in post-war Newcastle provided the impetus for the creation of the College of Art and Industrial Design which would eventually bring together a number of extant vocational courses already offered, but which also had great ambitions of providing training in all fields of design (College of Art and Industrial Design, 1955) (*see Figures 2 and 3*). Wendy attended the illustration and textile course (NDD), in the college in Clayton Road in the early 1950s where the facilities were crammed into a pair of Victorian semi-detached villas. However, Wendy, like many designers from the region, got the essential start from which she gradually developed the international reputation as one of the country's leading jewellery and metalwork designers. With the support of Newcastle City council, most notably sympathetic councillors Lipman and Squires, the principal of the COID, Cecil ("Seth") Smith was able to appoint key staff and develop throughout the 1960s and 1970s. The college quickly established a leading role both regionally and nationally, especially in the fields of graphic, fashion and three-dimensional design[5] (later to be split into DFI and 3D). Fine art at Northumbria was developed in response to the Coldstream requirements that art should inform all teaching in both art and design. Coldstream also required diploma courses to have at least 15% of study in the academic areas of complementary studies and Art history.[6] An early appointment was Mary Bromly to head the Fashion courses. From 1953 until retirement in 1992 she developed a range of innovative courses. Fashion became a major course with close links to high street and retail and gained an outstanding reputation (*see Figure 4*).The college's Graphic and Three-Dimensional design courses were validated for Dip AD status in the first punitive round. The consolidation of the disparate sections of Rutherford College and the COID was achieved in 1971–72 with the opening of Squires Building. Squires was planned as a purpose-built art school on a prestigious site opposite the Civic Centre. It was referred to as the "jewel in the Crown", by the proud Chairman of

Newcastle Education committee, Councillor Cyril Lipman. Lipman, a keen supporter of the Polytechnic ideal, had worked to ensure that the college became the School of Art and Design, Newcastle Polytechnic (*see Figure 5*). With its new building and Polytechnic status the School was set to expand and gain Dip AD and subsequently degree status for all its major Design, Fine Art, Photography and Media courses. John Elliott, appointed in 1972 from a design consultancy, was impressed with the facilities and accommodation which matched or even exceeded those in the industry. By the 1980s the School was one of the largest centres for Art and Design Education in Britain. Fine art grew rapidly in size and reputation and by 1974 Newcastle Polytechnic was awarding a Degree in FA, and a degree in the History of Modern Art and Design, one of the first such courses in Britain.

Student Achievement

The growing national and international reputation of Fine Art at Newcastle University and increasingly the Polytechnic shifted the student intake from mainly local to national (and international). Many graduates are now leading figures in the art and design world and beyond. Fine Art students from the earlier phase are known world wide. Sean Scully and Mark Lancaster are now both based in the USA, but exhibit worldwide. Tania Kovats, a Northumbria Fine Art graduate, who won the Barclays Young Contemporaries prize in 1991, later caused controversy with "Virgin in a condom" in New Zealand. Both she and the Turner Prize nominee Jane Wilson (with her sister Louise) have international reputations but have also participated in the North East art scene. Design graduates too have leading positions in some of the best known global companies. Here the designers may not be known by name to the public, but have created designs for Gap, Louis Vitton, Ford, Jaguar and other leading brands. Even in an industry where few designers become household names, Jonathan Ive has become a widely recognized name. His work for Apple, creating the iMac, iPod, and now the iPhone, surely mean that he is the graduate whose work is most likely to be owned and recognized by a wide range of consumers.

Peter Horbury is now Design Director for Ford North America, a remarkable achievement for a British designer. He previously worked with Volvo and Ford Europe, where his team transformed the image of Volvo with more affordable and less stodgy models such as the S40 and XC90, which have brought Volvos to a new generation. With Ford's take over of Volvo he led the design team on many of the new Ford designs. Another Design for Industry student, Simon Butterworth, has worked on design for Jaguar "S" type and recently worked on BMW's new "Euro" motorbike the Funduro. As design becomes increasingly involved in ideas, communication and team strategies it often becomes harder to identify single named designers in the traditional sense. Northumbria graduates are more likely to work under the banner of a corporate brand or consultancy. One exceptional success is Tim Brown, now CEO of the major international consultancy, IDEO. IDEO and many other firms now staffed by design graduates offer student placements, an important link with benefits for industry, the University and the individual student.

Of course not every art and design student will follow that career path. Many are better known for their achievements in other areas. Brian Ferry, like so many art students of his and subsequent generations became famous as a musician. Scott Henshall is better known to the public for his appearance in *I'm a celebrity, get me out of here!* (ITV, 2006), though he was already established in fashion through his statement dresses for celebrities such as Victoria Beckham and Kylie Minogue. Lowri Turner was recruited to journalism before she had even completed her degree in Fashion and is now better known as a TV presenter. The post-war "art school tradition" which created conditions of creative freedom, encouraged questioning, analytical and critical skills which would now be referred to as "transferable", is often credited for the outpouring of talent that have done so much to foster the enormous "creative industry" section of the British economy.

The intellectual, critical and analytical skills that distinguish these degree level courses are invaluable in designers' later careers and evident in the symposium, conference and presentations they are frequently called on to deliver. Peter Horbury, Tim Brown and Terry Farrell are all conspicuous examples of designers who contribute debate in international design forums. Another outstanding example of an articulate designer is Jonathan Ive, who has become Senior Vice-President for Industrial Design at Apple Computers. Ive has proved time and again his sympathy for material and function in the success of his intuitive design skills honed by full use of his training. In an era when the "hero" designer is often a myth, where team work is essential, Jonathan can still produce unique distinctive creation that is recognisable an "Ive" design. To hear Jonathan Ive talk about the design process is inspirational; some idea of the persuasiveness is conveyed in the various TV interviews he has given, such as when he won the Design Museum's "Designer of the Year" award in 2003. However, even more outstanding were his talks to workshop discussions with design students when he returned to Northumbria – unforgettable for the students involved.

On the whole, the design school system recognises and reinforces the primacy of London as *the* centre of activity. The fashion schools all try to show in London. "New designers", an annual exhibition of graduating student work from British Design courses, is deemed absolutely essential to showcase work to prospective employers. The students have to raise the thousands of pounds worth of funding needed to hire the stands, and pack and ship their work. Hopefully they will be singled out and offered employment. Of course it does happen, and for some, such as recent Three-Dimensional Design graduate Max Lamb, the world seems to fall at their feet. But important jobs are almost always in London or abroad. There have been exceptions to this pattern. One was the student of the remarkable furniture tutor Han Elleflaadt, Jeremy Pearce. He founded the Newcastle Furniture Company, which has progressed:

> ...*from two men and a dog, to now having more than 40 employees. We started off doing one-off pieces, and received funding from the crafts council section of the Arts Council, to exhibit in exhibitions alongside some of the top designer craftsmen in the UK, who were showing ceramics, fabrics, furniture and glass. "We ended up specialising in custom-made, top end kitchen furniture, and that now accounts for 85% of what we produce". (King, 2005: 28)*

Another is Nigel Cabourn, who with his company Cricket Clothing has remained a major force in fashion from his Newcastle base. However, in design, until very recently they were exceptions to the mass annual exodus of graduates from the North East. Can designers too, following the growing trend in the fine arts, retain a base in the North East?

Critical mass

The 1996 edition of *Northern Review* reflected on the 1960s art scene in Newcastle. Artists exhibited where they could, in pubs, theatre foyers, or made a brave attempt at establishing a gallery. Mostly if they wanted to exhibit they left the city and the North East, usually for good. However, this situation began to change, slowly at first in the 1970s, gathering pace in the 1980s and more so in the 1990s. The 1996 year of Visual Arts demonstrated, perhaps surprisingly the quantity, quality, and above all the *audience* for the arts in the North-East. John Walker's account of his student days in the 1950s confirms this account. In his early years as a tutor in Newcastle Tom Bromly with the "Newcastle Group" exhibited in the foyer of the Odeon Cinema; the green room of the People's

Theatre and in Fenwick's furniture store! But by the 1970s they had a more permanent space, which they in turn sublet to a new network of artists who called themselves "the basement group". This association of performance artists, mostly from Newcastle Polytechnic but also Newcastle University and Sunderland built on a series of exhibitions and "happenings" that drew artists and journalists internationally to Newcastle. Students and ex-students through the 1980s and 1990s gradually laid the planks for a fully functional local "art world"; magazines, performance events and a growing number of galleries all provided the essential infrastructure to enable artists to sell their work, and (perhaps just as importantly) create an artistic "atmosphere" of support, criticism and appreciation. The Polytechnic's Squires Gallery, became a permanent exhibition space, adding to the Hatton as a venue for new shows. Artist's groups such as Spectro gained Arts Council finding and grew into the Westgate Arts Centre. By 1996, the Year of the Visual Arts, there were dozens of galleries and even more temporary spaces. In the late 1990s this critical mass was further encouraged by the studio spaces becoming available, as industrial building began to be converted. In the Ouseburn Valley a charitable trust was able to obtain grants funding to convert the old Maling Pottery factory into artist's spaces, which included a gallery.

These spaces, where artists share some services, are available at an affordable rent. They make the – once almost impossible – leap from student to working artist possible. Now design students too have the possibility of setting up, post-degree, in a supportive environment. The list of membership of "Designed and Made", reveals many graduates from North-East art and design courses. *Design Works* in Gateshead was an early project providing this space for companies, Octo Design, an early tenant is now a major design company. The Ouseburn Trust is committed to and reliant on the creative and art industries for the sympathetic regeneration of the Valley. Project North East, a company which works to provide suitable premises for fledgling companies, has redeveloped Pink Lane in sympathy with the scale and atmosphere of that historic part of central Newcastle. Terry Farrell, world class architect, is working on "a cultural quarter", to link Newcastle University's museum and gallery facilities to the core of the city.

Outside commentators detect a massive revival of Newcastle/Gateshead as a cultural centre. They, of course, point mainly to the very visible Baltic and Sage Gateshead centres. However, for all the hundreds, thousands even, of students of art and design in the region, these are just the icing on the cake. For them the small, even individual, help is perhaps more valuable. The Arts Council has given valuable and consistent help. *One NorthEast* has schemes, large and small. One scheme at Northumbria University is the "Hatchery", which has supported graduates with business ideas. *Deadgood*, with its shop and presence in design exhibitions, is one such supported business run by recent graduates in Three-Dimensional Design. Another is *Zest Innovation*, a Service Design Consultancy, which started in the Hatchery and was able to move out into "real world" operation with support from NESTA. Its co-founder Laura Williams freely acknowledges their early support but also stressed the importance of networks in establishing their business. The creation of these networks: between artists, designers, agencies, galleries, the press, and of course the wider public as purchasers and audience, are what make it possible to say, with some confidence, that we now have a functional art-world in the North East.

The crucial phase in this development is not really the moment when students choose to stay and set up their own company. It is when they, in turn, take in new students for placements, passing on their networks and contacts. There is now a design forum to introduce students to potential employers through informal social events. The design company Indigo is international:

> But we always look to the North-East when we recruit because there are so many talented graduates coming through the universities in the region. It is a cliche, but we look locally and think nationally. "Newcastle always had a huge amount of talent to develop, and it was always on the verge of harnessing it. But the reality has been for a very long time now that people study for three years in the city, spent a year trying to find a job, and then go down to London where they can find work. "Things are starting to turn round now. You only have to look at the Angel of the North, the Quayside, Millennium Bridge, Baltic and of course the Sage. "They combine into a critical mass. It is happening now". (Anderson, 2003: 30)

In conclusion, of course it was not the Art and Design colleges alone which created the "critical mass" that characterises today's thriving creative scene in the North East. However, undoubtedly the staff and students of Art and Design courses have been crucial. The first generation of staff brought new ideas, energy and experience of a wider art and design world. Their contacts brought leading designers and artists to teach in the North East. The second generation, often the best students, stayed as teachers or if they pursued careers returned, often on a regular basis to teach or share experience with the current cohort. Though not discussed here the newer subjects of performance, media and now multi-media have also been developed at Northumbria University where students too have made major contributions internationally, nationally and to the region's visual culture and wider reputation. It seems timely to review this major contribution when these courses increasingly struggle to justify their unique identities and individuality in the now huge institutions that Newcastle and Northumbria Universities have become.

Notes

1. It should be noted that both Universities claim origins in the Government School of Design founded in 1842. That is too complicated an argument to engage with here. Allen and Buswell (2005) gives much detail of the precursor colleges of the University and the wrangling between that and the University.
2. On this course Itten wrote: 'The foundation of my design teaching was the general theory of contrast. Light and dark, material and texture studies, form and colour theory, rhythm and expressive forms were discussed and presented in their contrasting effects' (Itten, 1964: 12).
3. At the time he was unaware that it originated at the Bauhaus (Walker, 2003: 12).
4. Walker also noted there was little contact: 'I remember only one tutorial from Pasmore in my final year and I had to arrange it myself. Hamilton …was a printmaker as well as a painter he began to offer evening classes to students who wanted to learn printing techniques' (Walker, 2003: 11).
5. The Three-Dimensional Design course, originally incorporating both craft-like design and more industrial forms of design was later to be split into two. The component that concentrated on furniture and jewellery retained the title Three Dimensional Design, while a new course on Design for Industry emerged from the other aspects of the earlier course.
6. A requirement for Art and Design History also continued as the Diplomas were revalidated as degrees from 1971 by the CNAA' (Ashwin, 1975).

Acknowledgements

A number of people kindly agreed to be interviewed. This information was invaluable in providing specific and general background for this research.
My thanks especially to Tom and Mary Bromly, Stephanie Brown, Richard Bott, John Elliot, Douglas MacLennan, Jack Slade and Laura Williams.

Bibliography

Allen, J. & Buswell, R. (2005) *Rutherford's Ladder: the Making of Northumbria University, 1871-1996.* Newcastle: Northumbria University Press.

Anderson, G. (2003) 'Focusing on talent locally', *The Journal* (Newcastle), November 10, p. 30.

Ashwin, C. (1975) *Art Education: documents and policies 1768-1975.* London: SRHE.

College of Art and Industrial Design (1955) City and County of Newcastle upon Tyne Education Committee, Official Opening ...14th October: not paginated.

Frayling, C. (1987) *The Royal College of Art.* London: Barrie& Jenkins.

Hamilton, R. (1966) *'Interview with Victor Willing',* Studio International, September.

Itten, J. (1964) *Design and Form.* London: Thames & Hudson.

King, G. (2005) 'Awards Boost for top furniture firm', *The Journal* (Newcastle).

Macdonald, S. (1970) *The History and Philosophy of Art Education.* London: University of London Press.

Scott, M. (1996) 'Post-War Developments in Art in Newcastle: was it a Golden Age?', *Northern Review,* n. 4.

Strand, R. (1987) *A Good Deal of Freedom: Art and Design in the public sector of higher education, 1960-1982.* London: CNAA.

Thistlewood, D. (1981) *A Continuing Process: Creativity in British Art Education 1955-65.* London: ICA.

Walker, J. (2003) *Learning to Paint: A British Art Student and Art School 1956-61.* London: Institute of Artology.

Part Two

Film and Television

Chapter Five

Traditions and Transformations: Cinematic Visions of Tyneside

Peter Hutchings

Tyneside Phantasmagoria

On the High Level Bridge over the River Tyne, a gangster is beating up a woman. On the same bridge, a ruthless American businessman not averse to the use of violence himself is striking a deal with a jazz-loving Newcastle nightclub owner who bears more than a passing resemblance to the rock star Sting. Meanwhile, a short walk away along the Newcastle Quayside, a man and woman are standing on the altogether more modern Millennium Bridge. There is no violence this time, just a sense of romantic possibility as the couple contemplates the half-finished conversion of the Baltic Mill on the Gateshead side of the Tyne into an international arts centre. A group of women celebrating the successful transformation of their own lives are also about to step onto the same bridge from the Newcastle side. Further back into Gateshead, in-between the High Level and Millennium Bridges, is a bleak multi-story car park. From the side of this, the same gangster beating up the woman on the High Level Bridge is throwing a local businessman to his death, while two local teenagers at the very top stare longingly across the Tyne at the St James' Park football stadium, and also address some comments to the distant Gateshead-based Angel of the North, which since its installation in 1998 has become as iconic of the North-East as the Tyne Bridge. If these boys could see far enough, they might even glimpse themselves nestled at the base of the Angel, alongside the man from the Millennium Bridge, all of them caught up in a moment of masculine contemplation.

This is Tyneside on film, or at least a particular version of it. It might all be jumbled up, with images from the 1970s mingling with those from the 1980s and 2000s and with the architecture of the Tyne undergoing significant transformation from one moment to the next. However, these images are all linked together not just through their location near the Tyne itself but also through the way in which they present private dramas played out before, and in relation to, public spaces, buildings and monuments. This is Tyneside represented then in terms of an urban spectacle against which the narratives of the various films take place. It is a strategy associated most with films that have sought to introduce Tyneside – and Newcastle in particular – to audiences outside of the North East (and sometimes outside Great Britain as well) as a setting that is both novel and fascinating. Hence what might be termed a touristic emphasis on such visually appealing public sites as the Tyne and High Level Bridges, the redeveloped Newcastle Quayside, the Baltic, the Millennium Bridge, and the Angel of the North.

Other Tyneside-based films – notably those made by the Amber Collective – have generally eschewed this reliance on spectacle in favour of an engagement with characters in less familiar and less visually pleasing settings and situations. (See Hochscherf and Leggott in this volume for a discussion of Amber.) It does not follow that the mainstream commercial films with which this chapter will be dealing offer by contrast an exterior or outside view of Tyneside, as opposed to the local and potentially more realistic or authentic views offered by the likes of Amber. On the contrary, a number of these commercial mass-market films were produced by regionally based companies or involved regionally based cast and crew. In any event, the presentation of Tyneside in terms of widely circulated spectacular imagery clearly resonates with the various civic attempts that have been made within Tyneside over the past four decades to remodel the area's image in response to the decline of its traditional manufacturing industrial base and its gradual replacement by service industries. Again, it will not do simply to collapse these films into, or see them as a mere symptom of, this process of urban reconstruction. The films are not part of this or propaganda for it, but they do respond to it and trace its changing visual configurations within their own dramas.

The films to be discussed here include *Get Carter* (1971, d. Mike Hodges), *Stormy Monday* (1988, d. Mike Figgis), *Purely Belter* (2000, d. Mark Herman), *Gabriel and Me* (2001, d. Udayan Prasad), *The One and Only* (2002, d. Simon Cellan Jones) and *School for Seduction* (2004, d. Sue Heel). Importantly, they are all genre films, and their connection with Tyneside is mediated through whether they are, variously, crime thrillers, romantic comedies or social realist dramas (or combinations thereof). It follows that the clash of tones set up in the opening of this chapter – with scenes of violence conjoined with moments of humour and tenderness – is as much a clash of generic conventions as it is a reflection of changing times on Tyneside. In a sense, the real subject of this chapter will turn out to be the transaction between particular genres and a changing Tyneside, with that relationship requiring both a local knowledge of Tyneside's public spaces and sites and an ability to deploy those spaces and sites within stock genre narratives in a manner that has significance and meaning beyond Tyneside itself. What might therefore initially appear to be a developmental move from a brutal masculinist crime ridden 1970s – exemplified by *Get Carter* – to a more hopeful and transformative presentation of contemporary Tyneside is, in fact, more complex, and the uses of parts of Tyneside as locations more various, than has sometimes been supposed, with an apparent 1970s brutality qualified in many ways and modern fantasies of personal transformation more limited than they first appear. If nothing else, the films to be discussed here have captured and explored some of the ambiguities and ambivalences that have arisen from a changing

Tyneside and in particular the difficult relation between tradition and transformation, but they have all done so from perspectives not limited to the North East region itself.

Crime on the Tyne

The gangster film *Get Carter* is a key point of reference for cinematic representations of Tyneside, if only because it has been seen so widely and has acquired a substantial cult following. However, the fact remains that its location in Tyneside was something of an afterthought. *Jack's Return Home*, the novel by Ted Lewis from which the film was adapted, was set in an unnamed small town that has since been identified by critics as Scunthorpe. The transposition of this grim revenge drama to Tyneside was the end result of a location trawl along the East Coast of England by the film's director Mike Hodges and its producer Michael Klinger. Hodges himself later explained his reason for choosing Newcastle over what had been his initial choice, Hull.

> *We passed on and came to Newcastle. The visual drama of the place took my breath away. Seeing the great bridges crossing the Tyne, the waterfront, the terraced houses stepped up each side of the deep valley, I knew that Jack was home. And although the developers were breathing down the Scotswood Road, they hadn't yet gobbled it up. We'd got there in time. But only just. (Cited in Chibnall, 2003: 24–25)*

This fascination with the visual-poetic possibilities of an industrial town clearly connects with a similar fascination evident in the British New Wave films of the early 1960s. For instance, films such as *Saturday Night and Sunday Morning* (1960, d. Karel Reisz) and *A Kind of Loving* (1962, d. John Schlesinger) captured an industrial reality that was both gritty and picturesque, while the Tyneside-set thriller *Payroll* (1961, d. Sidney Hayers) – part of an early 1960s cycle of New Wave-influenced crime films – did something comparable with Newcastle itself (for a discussion of New Wave crime films, see Chibnall, 1999.) Such an approach arguably sets up tensions between a desire to explore the reality of a particular industrial environment from within and a concern to view it, and indeed aestheticise it, from an external perspective, and much subsequent critical work on the New Wave has focused on its ambiguous representations of working-class reality.

Within such a context, the fact that Michael Caine, in the role of Newcastle-bred gangster Jack Carter returned home to avenge his brother's death, does not even attempt a Geordie accent but speaks instead in his native London tones, begins to make sense. The director Mike Hodges has suggested that Carter had lost his local accent after he had relocated to London (Chibnall, 2003: 27). Whether or not one finds this credible as an explanation of his character, Caine's London accent does effectively mark him as an outsider to Newcastle, albeit one that is bound to the city by ties of blood and family history; in this way, Carter – as the local boy returning home after some time away – helps to articulate the film's own insider-outsider relationship to Tyneside itself.

Another point of possible connection between the New Wave and *Get Carter*, albeit a less obvious one, is a shared thematic preoccupation with masculine identity in the face of social change. In the case of the New Wave, this manifested itself in a fascination with new hedonistic male lifestyles that were evolving in a situation of increasing affluence. However, this was often counter-posed to negatively-presented forms of domestic consumption that were associated with femininity and which threatened the freedom of the men, with the railing of male protagonists against what they perceived as their entrapment often acquiring a misogynistic quality (see Hill, 1986: 127–176 for a discussion of the films in these terms). *Get Carter* can be seen as an extremely degraded version of this. Undoubtedly, misogyny permeates the world conjured up by the film, with Carter himself particularly brutal in his treatment of women. What is missing is the attractive energy of the New Wave protagonists, for Carter remains – for all the recent "laddish" attempts to valorize him as an icon of British masculinity – a deeply unattractive and dysfunctional figure. He is associated with death from the film's beginning (although the film does not underline it, the hit man who will eventually kill him is travelling in the same railway carriage as him on his journey from London to Newcastle) and his few displays of emotion lead almost immediately to outbursts of violence. Perhaps more importantly, Carter is clearly signalled as a redundant figure, as someone whose unforgiving values are being swept away and who has no place in this world, hence the inevitability of his death.

It is Carter who is beating up the woman on the High Level Bridge and throwing a businessman off the Gateshead multi-story car park. In both cases, the architecture correlates to Carter in a shared unyielding hardness. This is particularly so with the High Level Bridge, a nineteenth century Robert Stephenson-designed construction that functions as a monumental reminder of

Newcastle's proud industrial history. However, Carter himself, while on the bridge, describes Newcastle with some bitterness as a "crap house", and there is precious little evidence of industrial activity, or any kind of legitimate work, elsewhere in the film. A comparable sense of a construction no longer connected with contemporary Tyneside is evident in the more modern and less architecturally distinguished Gateshead car park (which at the time of writing this chapter has finally been scheduled for demolition). The businessman murdered by Carter is in the process of constructing an up-market restaurant on top of the car park and, as if to underline the way in which this reflects an affluence rising up from the South of the country, he has hired two effete Southern designers to this end. He is, in Carter's words, "a big man but... in bad shape", and what is perceived as his softness and his domestication serve not only to distinguish him from the ultra-hard Carter but also ally him with a future more dependent on conspicuous consumption and social aspiration than it is on industrial work (or the kind of gangsterism embodied by Carter as a degraded equivalent of manual labour). A comparison might be drawn here with the popular Newcastle-set television situation comedy *Whatever Happened to the Likely Lads* (1973–74), in which the forward-looking Bob was the aspirational figure fully attuned to all the social nuances of patterns of consumption while the more retrograde Terry was an old-fashioned Carter-like figure ill-suited to the new world of affluence and social pretension (see Hutchings, 1996.)

It seems from this that, for all its casual male brutality, *Get Carter* does not actually present Tyneside, and Newcastle in particular, in terms of "sexism and patriarchal organisational hierarchies" (a phrase used by Claire Monk to describe 1970s British gangland dramas: Monk, 2000a, 280) but instead as a location that is, in Mike Hodges's words, "on the cusp" (*Get Carter* DVD commentary), where new patterns of consumption and taste are gradually making their presence known. Social change is in the air, and while one would have to look very hard to find any positive or progressive representations of women here, the men are far from glamourised and are generally presented as unattractive or dysfunctional. Accordingly, the city that gave birth to hard man Carter also turns out to be the city that does away with him.

It is interesting to leap ahead 17 years to *Stormy Monday*, another Tyneside-set crime thriller, albeit one with a very different set of emphases. Like much of 1980s British cinema, it has been seen as a reaction against elements of Thatcherism, and indeed *Stormy Monday* does offer a critique of unbridled capitalism, especially as represented by the attempts of a ruthless American businessman to buy up sections of Newcastle. It also presents a decidedly jaundiced view of Anglo-US political relations, with photographs of Margaret Thatcher and Ronald Reagan gracing a civic ceremony welcoming the villainous businessman to town. *Get Carter* contained a few hints about civic corruption, but it was made some years before the architect John Poulson and Newcastle councillor T. Dan Smith were jailed for corruption in a blaze of negative publicity for the city, and in any event *Get Carter*'s principal focus was on Carter's revenge rather than on Newcastle itself. By contrast, the post-Poulson *Stormy Monday* was able to represent a clearer sense of local civic institutions undergoing quiet and subtle corruption at the hands of the businessman-villain Frank Cosmo (played by Tommy Lee Jones), while the city itself is shown to be thoroughly infiltrated by American capital and American culture. The film is set during Newcastle's "America Week", and visual references to American culture – a large Pepsi bottle installed in the street, bouncers dressed as US police officers – abound.

What might appear to be a straightforward case of anti-Americanism, as canny locals see off the foreign invaders, turns out to be more complex, however. As both Charlotte Brunsdon and John Hill have noted, the film draws heavily on US film noir for its visuals and US music for its soundtrack:

> *Although Cosmo, despite the recognition that it is not appropriate to 'go round acting like Al Capone', may be too American a villain to be permitted to actually buy the quayside, in a sense, in a movie in thrall to the Hollywood cinema and the Blues, it is already his. (Brunsdon, 1999: 158–59; also see Hill, 1999)*

It is also the case that the local forces arrayed against Cosmo are less "local" or insular than the inhabitants of Newcastle in *Get Carter*. Finney (played by Sting) is a shady nightclub owner whose defiant response to America Week is to book a Polish jazz band but who is willing to do a deal with Cosmo if the price is right (with this deal being struck on the High Level Bridge). By contrast, Brendan (played by Sean Bean) is younger and more naive but he has travelled to the United States and during the film expresses his desire to return there; he also acquires an American girlfriend, albeit of part-Polish extraction (played by Hollywood star Melanie Griffiths). It seems from this that *Stormy Monday* is thoroughly imbued with cross-cultural and transnational qualities, both in terms of its characterisations and its visual and aural style, with this all associated in turn with a troubled modernisation of the space of Newcastle. This reflects the film's status as a British version of an American-based genre, the gangster picture (just as *Get Carter* contains numerous references to its American counterparts and indeed has itself been remade as an American production on two occasions). Again we are confronted with an intermingling of local and national/international perspectives, and a fascination with Tyneside that at the same time seeks to locate this in relation to extra-regional themes and concerns. Newcastle might have become more visually appealing and more cosmopolitan in *Stormy Monday* than it is in *Get Carter*, but the same sense of a traditional industrial identity gradually giving way to forces and trends from outside the city is evident within both films. The fact that these are crime films ensures that the tensions involved in this process of social change are represented in terms of transgression and violence. Later films in other genres would address similar issues in a different way.

Transformations on the Tyne

If traditional identities seemed impossible to jettison entirely in *Get Carter* and *Stormy Monday*, identity was apparently more malleable in a recent small group of feature films produced on Tyneside, including *Purely Belter, Gabriel and Me, School for Seduction* and *The One and Only*. The first three of these clearly belong to, and were marketed in terms of, a pre-existing cycle of dramas dealing with the fate of men in a post-industrial world: the best-known of these are probably *Brassed Off* (1996), *The Full Monty* (1997) and *Billy Elliot* (2000). *Purely Belter* came from the same director as *Brassed Off, Gabriel and Me* was written by *Billy Elliot*-writer Lee Hall, and *School for Seduction* was sold as a female version of *The Full Monty*.

While immensely popular, films such as *The Full Monty* and *Billy Elliot* have been criticised both for offering fantasy-based individualistic solutions to real social problems and for prioritising masculine concerns in a manner that potentially has misogynist connotations. For example, Claire Monk has argued that *The Full Monty* and *Brassed Off*:

> ...*transformed the problems of male unemployment and social exclusion and related psychic crises into incongruously feel good comedy ...films consistently and pointedly expressed the problems of the post-industrial male in a "feminised" society as problems of gender, rather than economic relations. (Monk, 2000b: 159–60)*

The contribution made by Tyneside-based films to this cycle turned out to be comparatively muted and did not achieve the commercial success of the earlier films. However, these films do possess distinctive qualities that can be seen to derive from recent changes in the Tyneside landscape. In particular, the installation of the Angel of the North, the conversion of the Baltic Mill, the construction of the Millennium Bridge, and the wider redevelopment of the Quayside manifest themselves in these films as signs of civic transformation that provide a suitable backdrop for more personal dramas of transformation.

Purely Belter is especially interesting in this respect. An early sequence shows the two male teenagers who will be the film's main protagonists sitting on top of the Gateshead multi-story car park that featured in *Get Carter*. Their main focus is on the St James' football stadium in Newcastle, with this representing – as it does in *The One and Only*, where one of the characters plays for Newcastle United – an ideal site for male aspiration (it is where the boys want to be) but also a site of male performance, display and vanity that is in some ways – again notably in *The One and Only* – perceived as "unmanly". Also from their vantage point on top of the car park, the boys can see the Angel of the North, which they characterise as feminine (although, famously, the sculpture was modelled on sculptor Antony Gormley's own body) and as their own personal "guardian angel". The symbolic nature of what in effect is a gendered juxtaposition of two public monuments is underlined by its sheer impossibility, for in reality the Angel is not visible from the car park, and in order to achieve the desired juxtaposition the film-makers had to digitally implant the Angel into a landscape where it did not actually belong.

Both *Purely Belter* and *Gabriel and Me* – the latter of which makes less use of Newcastle's public spaces – centre on young male protagonists with caring and understanding mothers (or angels, if one follows *Purely Belter*'s symbolism) and difficult fathers. In *Purely Belter*, Gerry's father is a violent, abusive figure whose accidental death at the film's conclusion offers hope for the future, while Jimmy's father in *Gabriel and Me* is unemployed, dying from cancer, deeply embittered (perhaps understandably), and incapable of understanding his son's flights of imagination and desire to become an angel. Although he is presented much more sympathetically than Gerry's monster of a father, both are firmly associated with Newcastle's industrial past, especially in their old-fashioned and male-centred chauvinism, a quality that is comprehensively rejected by their offspring. In a sense, both fathers are Jack Carter-like figures who do not belong in a contemporary post-industrial Tyneside but whose troubling presence lingers on.

The transformations undergone by the young male protagonists of *Purely Belter* and *Gabriel and Me* are less triumphant than that experienced by the men in *The Full Monty* or Billy in *Billy Elliot*. Instead, they seem to involve little more than a coming to terms with the father's defunct values, with the boys in each film left in the same position of social marginality as they were at the beginning, albeit with a slightly more hopeful future. As for the long-suffering mothers, they remain as idealised and unchanging as the Angel itself. In these films at least, the future seems to be male.

School for Seduction could be seen as an antidote to all this male-centredness if it were not for the fact that it struggles to convert a *Full Monty*-like narrative into something that convincingly works for female characters. It could be argued that within a patriarchal context the theme of post-industrial male social disempowerment presents opportunities for an affirmative restoration of a secure male identity that retrospectively designates the original disempowerment as aberrant. Male power and dominance is thereby made to appear as a natural state of affairs. It is harder to do this with female characters given that the idea of female social disempowerment possesses much greater political weight and historical resonance and has been a focus for debate and action over many decades. Accordingly, the transformations experienced by the women in *School for Seduction* – involving the dumping of unpleasant male partners or the humiliation of an unpleasant male boss – seem rather trite and petty given the seriousness of the issues they raise about spousal abuse and exploitative employment conditions for women. Bearing this in mind, it is fitting that the film's central transformation involves a Newcastle woman magically changing her identity through the simple expedient of pretending to be an Italian. *School for Seduction* ends with its female characters walking out onto the Millennium Bridge and towards the Baltic. Civic transformation thus becomes the women's transformation too, although their empowerment is perhaps too easily won to be meaningful.

Something comparable is going on in the romantic comedy *The One and Only*, which boasts impeccable local credentials inasmuch as it was written by Peter Flannery and directed by Simon Cellan Jones, who together had been responsible for the critically acclaimed Newcastle-based television series *Our Friends in the North*. By contrast, *The One and Only* was perceived by critics as offering a more fantasy-based version of Tyneside as an exciting and recently remodelled location. "The Tyne bridge, or the Millennium bridge, or the Angel of the North are pedantically visible in almost every shot" complained one critic (*The Guardian*, 21 February 2003).

What is striking about *The One and Only*, for the purposes of this chapter at least, is the way that it encapsulates, knowingly or otherwise, key themes evident in other cinematic representations of Tyneside over the past 40 years. Neil, its central male protagonist, is the very model of the disempowered post-industrial new man. He is in touch with his emotions: "He's warm and spontaneous. Very unusual in a man from around here," comments his sister-in-law. Even his trade associates him with a feminising domesticity for he is a kitchen fitter who works for his ambitious and aspirational wife. Unfortunately, he also has a low sperm count and is unable to father a child. "My dad was the same," he jokes. As this is a rom-com, this kind of disempowerment does not carry the weight of the disempowerment of the men in the likes of *The Full Monty* but it is something to which the film does attend, initially through rather callously removing Neil's wife via a fatal road accident and subsequently through finding him a more suitable partner.

Like Neil's wife, Stevie, the film's main female protagonist, has some qualities that might be deemed "masculine". She is assertive and physically strong – successfully flattening her husband at the end of one argument – and not only has a male-sounding name but also has an Italian husband called Andrea, which to an English ear sounds like a woman's name. Stevie seems in fact to be as much a modern independent woman as Neil is a modern domesticated male, and it becomes the film's project to bring them together as an ideal couple through a series of absurd but predictable contrivances and in doing this to provide a comic view of post-industrial sexual politics. Particularly useful for this project is the refurbishment of the Baltic Mill that is ongoing throughout the film, for this becomes an image not just of the characters' own personal development but also of the general supplanting of tradition by something altogether more modern. It is appropriate therefore that Neil and Stevie's wedding reception at the end of the film takes place inside the now-finished Baltic.

The idea that Stevie's only possible trajectory is remarriage suggests that *The One and Only*'s conceptualisation of the independent woman is somewhat limited. However, undermining, or at least bringing some much-needed nuance to, what might appear to be a decidedly saccharine narrative is the presence of two other characters who shadow Neil and Stevie and provide connections to older ways of representing Tyneside. For Neil, it is Stan, an old-fashioned unsophisticated working-class male hopelessly out of place in the remodelled Newcastle, who is overwhelmingly associated with the body and base physical sensations, and who is thoroughly puzzled by the modern art that will eventually feature in the Baltic. Stevie's equivalent of Stan is the equally earthy Stella, who in the course of the film picks up Stan while late-night cruising in a supermarket. Their ensuing affair provides a rude counterpoint to Neil and Stevie's more decorous relationship and also arguably functions as an attenuated version of an unreconstructed Tyneside past that, for all the redevelopment of the Tyneside landscape, refuses to go away entirely.

Philip French commented thus on *The One and Only*'s use of its Tyneside location. "Every scene in this magical setting exudes promise and prosperity. The streets are clean and uncluttered. The traffic flows easily. From every window, there are magnificent vistas of the Tyne. Whenever the hero is faced with a problem, he sits beneath Antony Gormley's inspiring Angel of the North and finds peace." (*The Observer*, 24 February 2003.) French's words, which pay no attention to Stan or Stella, might be applied just as well to *School for Seduction* and even, to a certain extent, to *Purely Belter* as they present Tyneside as a veritable utopian site that has itself been remade and within which one can remake oneself. However, the brutal and degraded masculine world of *Get Carter* has not been entirely effaced from this landscape, and its traces can be found in some of these later films, in moments of crudity and violence, in a certain male-centredness, and in a tacit attachment to an industrial past.

There is a scene in *The One and Only* in which Neil and Stevie stand on the Millennium Bridge and admire the Baltic redevelopment. It is an archetypal expression of the new Tyneside – airy, light and modern and full of hope for the future. However, an inspection of the new Tyneside film suggests, if nothing else, that the past generally returns in some form or other. Neil and Stevie only have to turn around and they will find themselves looking at the High Level Bridge just a short way down the river. And perhaps the baleful ghost of Jack Carter will be looking back at them.

References

Brunsdon, C. (1999) 'Space in the British crime film', in S. Chibnall & R. Murphy (eds) *British Crime Cinema*. London: Routledge, pp. 148–159.

Chibnall, S. (1999) 'Ordinary people: "New Wave" realism and the British crime film 1959–1963', in S. Chibnall & R. Murphy (eds) *British Crime Cinema*. London: Routledge, pp. 94–109.

Chibnall, S. (2003) *Get Carter*. London: I.B. Tauris.

Hill, J. (1986) *Sex, Class and Realism: British Cinema, 1956–1963*. London: British Film Institute.

Hill, J. (1999) 'Allegorising the nation: British gangster films of the 1980s', in S. Chibnall & R. Murphy (eds) *British Crime Cinema*. London: Routledge, pp. 160–171.

Hutchings, P. (1996) 'When the going gets tough: Representations of the North East in film and television', in T. Faulkner. (ed.) *Northumbrian Panorama: Studies in the History and Culture of North East England*. London: Octavian Press, pp. 273–290.

Monk, C. (2000a) 'Underbelly UK: The 1990s underclass film, masculinity and the ideologies of "new" Britain', in J. Ashby & A. Higson (eds) *British Cinema, Past and Present*. London: Routledge, pp. 274–287.

Monk, C. (2000b) 'Men in the 90s', in R. Murphy (ed.) *British Cinema of the 90's*. London: British Film Institute.

Chapter Six

Visual and Embodied Pleasures: Cinema-going in Newcastle upon Tyne

Sarah Leahy

Over the last 5 years, and in Newcastle in particular, there has been a considerable evolution of the cinema-going landscape. Firstly, this can be seen in the power struggles for audience share between the multiplexes which are frequently located in out-of-town commercial centres (the Metrocentre, Silverlink) – with the one notable exception of the cinema at The Gate in Newcastle city centre. A second example is the restoration and development of the independent art-house venue, the Tyneside Cinema. In addition, the city has witnessed the development of 'microplex' exhibition venues (e.g. the Side, the Star and Shadow, the Little Jewel, the mobile cinema).

As a way of laying the foundations for an investigation of contemporary and historical cinema audiences in Tyneside, this chapter will chart the developments of three key exhibition venues in Newcastle: the Empire at the Gate (formerly the Odeon) (*see Figures 1 and 2*); the Tyneside Cinema (*see Figure 3*), an independent cinema specialising in art-house and foreign films; and the Star and Shadow cinema (*see Figures 4 and 5*), a community cinema built and run by volunteers. The key aim is to contribute to the understanding of the development of the cinematic landscape 100 years after the arrival of the first purpose-built cinemas in British towns and cities by offering a "micro-analysis" of particular venues over a relatively short period of time within one city. However, this analysis will be contextualised within the framework of existing scholarship on film cultures and cinema-going in Britain, on the one hand, and on the other, awareness of the historical dimension of cinema-going within Newcastle itself.[1]

Audience figures reached their peak in Britain in the immediate post-war period with 1,635 million entries recorded in 1946 (Doyle, 2003: 59). Even when these figures began to decline, Britain retained its position as the number one cinema-going nation well into the 1950s, with an average of twenty-eight visits per person per year. As Doyle points out, though, this figure does not offer a representation of the geographical fluctuations in cinema attendance: he cites Glasgow as the most film-loving city with fifty-one entries per person per year, closely followed by three industrial cities of Northern England: Newcastle upon Tyne, Manchester and Blackpool, all with fifty entries (Doyle, 2003: 61, figures are for 1952). Newcastle, therefore, has a history as one of the main centres of cinema-going in the North of England, where the industrial towns and cities drew in much higher audiences than in the South (with the exception of London).

Nationally speaking, the lowest point of cinema attendance was 1984, since when industry statistics chart a rise in audience figures of 135% over the next 10 years.

Once again, though, this global figure hides important regional variations: in the South East, South West, Wales and Scotland, growth has been minimal (ranging from 44% in Wales to 103% in Scotland) compared with what Doyle terms the "traditional heartlands of cinema", the North West (260%), North East (230%), Yorkshire and Humberside (197%), and the Midlands have emerged as a new cinematic centre (250%) (Doyle, 2003: 68).

Doyle follows "most commentators" (e.g. Eyles, 1997: 224–25; Gomery, 1992: 105) in attributing this reversal of fortunes since 1984 to the arrival of the multiplex – a persuasive argument given that the rise in attendances is strongest in those areas with the largest concentration of multiplex cinemas (the North West and the Midlands). While the arrival of multiplex cinemas has clearly been a boon in many ways to the British film industry at least at the level of exhibition, there have been accusations that these large out-of-town sites have come to dominate the market to an unhealthy extent – in fact limiting the choice of available films, failing to contribute to local economies, and endangering the existence of smaller independent cinemas, in particular outside of the large metropolitan centres of London, Birmingham, Manchester, Glasgow and Edinburgh (see Jancovich and Faire, 2003: 197–200; Harbord, 2002: 40). Eyles, however, hints that the rising audience figures are not solely confined to the multiplex sector, but that in fact, renewed interest in picture going may well benefit the non-mainstream, art-house sector too (Eyles, 1997: 225). It would certainly appear that since the mid-1990s, that is what has happened in Newcastle, where the independent sector has expanded and continues to develop, while the number of multiplex sites has been rationalised with the closure of the Warner Village cinema. The first part of this chapter will refer to recent work on film exhibition and audiences, in order to set out the theoretical framework for an examination of three different cinemas in Newcastle, with particular focus on the last 5 years, which will form the second and main part of this chapter.

Taste, Body and Space

Phil Hubbard, in an examination of the appeal of multiplex cinemas, has argued that leisure spaces in contemporary cities need to be seen not merely in terms of a binary divide between city centre and peripheral spaces each catering to different groups, but rather as "a patchwork of different leisure spaces, each of which is characterised by a distinctive set of embodied *practices* rather than distinctive audiences" (Hubbard, 2003: 270, original emphasis). Hubbard's article, based on the findings of a study of cinema audiences in Leicester, focuses on pleasures highlighted by his respondents as particular to the Warner Village out-of-town multiplex cinemas compared with the city centre variety – pleasures directly associated with their geographical location away from the city centre. What these responses show is that cinemas are chosen not solely (or even primarily) because of the film but that the exhibition site plays an important role in this choice. For example, Hubbard's respondents cited the Warner Village cinema as offering comfort, cleanliness, ease of parking, a sense of personal safety, clear organisation of space in the foyer (queuing systems and so on), all of which distinguished it from the city centre Odeon cinema which was associated with (potentially threatening) youth audiences, rowdy behaviour, dirt and a lack of parking facilities (Hubbard, 2003: 261–65). It is striking that the pleasures described here are not only (or even mainly) visual, but are experienced through and in the body.

The largely positive responses Hubbard encountered relating to Warner Village in Leicester are somewhat tempered by rather more critical reactions to the Showcase Cinema (also an out-of-town multiplex) in Nottingham recounted to Jancovich and Faire. For many of their respondents, embodied sensations are not solely, or even primarily pleasurable. The cinema is described as "cold" (literally and metaphorically), as smelling "funny" and as being pervaded by the sickly smell of popcorn (Jancovich and Faire, 2003: 205). In terms more than reminiscent of Bourdieu, Jancovich and Faire refer to the "visceral intolerance" that comes through in these descriptions – a phrase that could equally characterise some descriptions cited by Hubbard: "It's got sticky floors because of all the popcorn machines. It's really gross" (Sarah, 2001, describing the Odeon city centre multiplex); "noisy", "full of litter" (Pam, 2001), and "an overpowering smell of popcorn and hotdogs" (Catherine, 2001), both describing the out-of-own Warner Village (which as we have seen above, many of Hubbard's other respondents preferred because they found it to be clean). In *Distinction*, Bourdieu also makes this link between aesthetic taste and the body:

> ...*tastes are perhaps first and foremost distastes, disgust provoked by horror or visceral intolerance ("sick-making") of the tastes of others. (…) each taste feels itself to be natural – and so it almost is, being a habitus – which amounts to rejecting others as unnatural and therefore vicious. Aesthetic intolerance can be terribly violent. (Bourdieu, 1984: 56)*

Here, Bourdieu undoes the Kantian distinction between mind and body. While the audience experiences above can be seen as relating more directly to physical experience (smell, in particular is invoked as a particularly corporeal sense), it is important to recognise that the consideration of film cultures in terms of the use of exhibition sites requires us to conceive of the film viewer as embodied. This chimes with the work of Laura Marks (2000; 2002), Vivian Sobchak (1992), Steven Shaviro (1993) and others, which challenges the understanding of the relationship between film and spectator as a primarily visual experience, instead arguing for a phenomenological approach to our lived, embodied experience of the world. Such an approach cannot remain fixated upon texts as the primary site of spectatorial engagement with film, but demands a broader understanding of film culture that engages with the social and cultural experiences of the audience.

One of the main criticisms that have been levelled at Bourdieu's work is its apparent determinism. However, it does nonetheless have the merit of revealing aesthetic taste as constructed – and constructed in terms of difference (difference experienced corporeally as well as psychologically). And though the determinism of his work would seem to be at odds with Hubbard's performative notion of embodied practices, as Judith Butler's work on gender and sexuality has shown, conceptualising behaviour as performative – in terms of doing rather than being – does not necessarily dissociate it from social and cultural imperatives (Butler, 1990; 1993). Such imperatives are perhaps not so different from what Bourdieu terms the habitus – the structures of education, family and social class within which our tastes are shaped. The work of Harbord (2002) Hubbard (2003) and Jancovich and Faire (2003) emphasises the importance in film studies of recognising that it is not just the choice of films viewed that is determined by aesthetic taste, but that the choice of exhibition site is also a far from neutral decision, bound up as it is in the complex relationship between taste and social and cultural identity. And, as Harbord argues, this relationship needs to be viewed in terms of the tensions between institutional structures and individual agency (Harbord, 2002: 7). Consumption of films and the spaces in which they are shown, then, is regulated by the apparatus (understood as the technology of film production and projection, and in a broader sense of distribution and exhibition), but must also be seen in terms of a set of individual choices and practices. With this in mind, let us now move to a consideration of the three Newcastle sites.

Cinemas in Newcastle

The Empire is a multiplex cinema located within a commercial centre (The Gate) which also contains bars, restaurants and a casino (*see Figures 1 and 2*). Films are presented within this space as objects of consumption, interchangeable with other such objects. The Empire is keen to promote itself as being at the forefront of cinema projection technology. According to The Gate website: "Empire's state of the art cinema at The Gate has 12 screens ranging from 67 to 552 seats in size, all with Dolby Surround Sound and the capability to show any format of film". Beyond the usual ice-cream parlour, popcorn and sweets for sale in the foyer, there is little attempt here to attract customers into spending time within the cinema for any reason other than viewing a film – rather, the cinema is seen as one part of a larger complex where film-going is clearly identified as one leisure activity among many others – going to see a film is perhaps just part of a night out that also involves eating and drinking. Interestingly, this differs from the Odeon cinema at Silverlink, where there is a café featuring film memorabilia (as décor, but also for sale), as well as selling books, DVDs of recent popular films and CDs with a film connection. This not only capitalises on film-goers as potential consumers of associated merchandise, it also suggests that in this more self-contained venue, there is a recognition of the social practices associated with the activity of film-going.

The programme for the current week at the Empire includes: *The Number 23* (Schumacher, 2007); *Ghost Rider* (Johnson, 2007); *The Good Shepherd* (de Niro, 2006) including certain subtitled screenings; *Goal! 2: Living the Dream* (Collet-Serra, 2007); *Music and Lyrics* (Lawrence, 2007); *School for Scoundrels* (Phillips, 2006); *Material Girls* (Coolidge, 2007); *Charlotte's Web* (Winick, 2006); *Arthur et les Minimoys* (Besson, 2006); *Blood Diamond* (Zwick, 2006); *The Queen* (Frears, 2006); *Hannibal Rising* (Webber, 2007); *The Illusionist* (Burger, 2006), *Epic Movie* (Friedberg and Selzer, 2007), *Hot Fuzz* (Wright, 2007), *Freedom Writers* (La Gravenese, 2007), *Flushed Away* (Bowers and Fell, 2006) and *Night at the Museum* (Levy 2006). Here we note the predominance of comedies, thrillers and children's/family films, though there are films catering for older audiences (*The Good Shepherd, The Queen*) and although the presence of a foreign language film (*Arthur et les Minimoys*) is unusual, it is notable that it is a Luc Besson film – one of a few directors working in non-English language film to have conquered English-speaking multiplex territory.

The multiplex at The Gate, previously owned by Odeon Cinemas, was recently taken over by the Empire chain (in May 2006), with the Odeon preferring to concentrate their energies in the out-of-own Metrocentre and Silverlink (this is at odds with the Odeon's strategy in many other UK towns and cities, where the chain dominates the city centre multiplex market, often with cinemas in newly built leisure complexes just like The Gate). However, these shifts have taken place since the closure of the old Odeon located in Pilgrim Street in the centre of Newcastle. This old-style cinema, built originally for the Paramount chain in 1931 and taken over by Oscar Deutsch's Odeon cinemas in 1939, was for many years the premier first-run house in the city, used occasionally for concerts as well as film shows.[2] It was known for its technical innovation – it was the first picture house in Newcastle to introduce Cinemascope – as well as for its lavish decoration. The single auditorium (seating 2,600) was converted into a three-screen cinema in 1975, with the largest of the three accommodating 1,228 spectators. A fourth screen was added in 1980 bringing the total seating capacity to 1,997. The arrival of multiplex cinemas in Newcastle-Gateshead in 1987 with the opening of the ten screen AMC in the Gateshead Metrocentre (now the Odeon), and in 1989 with the Warner Village complex in Newcastle at Manors, just outside the city centre, did not immediately impact on the Odeon figures according to its manager of the time (Manders, 1991: 118). However, the Odeon cinemas eventually came to embrace the multi-screen format on a national level, and the Pilgrim Street building was sold in 2002, and the chain transferred their operation to the shiny new venue of the Gate which opened its doors in 2003.

Interestingly, the apparently happy co-existence of the Warner Village with the old-style Odeon cinema did not continue with the latter's move to the multiplex format. In spite of the apparent advantages of the Warner site over the city centre venue (free parking, cheaper tickets) and the Odeon's loss of its distinctive building and its spectacular large auditorium, it was The Gate site that won over audiences and the Warner Village was sold by Vue Cinemas to Northumbria University in 2004.

It would seem that the suburban location of Warner Village may have contributed to its downfall, unable to cater in the same way for the youth audience as the city centre facility, where the attractions of the multiplex are available in close proximity to those of the city, and in a location easily accessible by public transport. Given the constant supply of Hollywood films aimed principally at young male viewers such a venue is practically guaranteed success. The advantages boasted by the Warner Village site, then, would not necessarily have appeared as such to the youth audience. While car parking facilities may be important for older audiences and families, for people dependent on other forms of transport, not only does this not feature as a benefit but could in fact represent a distinct disadvantage. The location of the cinema in a car-dominated landscape is potentially alienating, and increases the isolation of the venue. The competition from a rival located not just close to the attractions of the city centre, but within a brand new leisure complex, was apparently then too much for the suburban Warner Village, which also had to compete with other, similar but newer out-of-town sites. Even its proximity to student halls of residence did not save it from closure. It will be interesting to continue to chart the progress of the Empire at The Gate. The impressive newness of the site has not lasted long and it is now strongly reminiscent of the descriptions cited by Hubbard of the city centre Odeon in Leicester (see earlier, Hubbard, 2003: 261). What is striking is that in spite of having already changed hands once in its short lifetime (an indication of the multiplexes' particular vulnerability to shifts in the global financial structures of the film industry) this does not seem to have impacted upon the audiences, suggesting that the branding of the space has little impact on its users (indeed, many of them appear unaware of the change).

If it is the case that one multiplex is very much like another, and it is their location with regard to the urban centre that determines their audience rather than any individual characteristics, this is not the case for the independent sector, where distinction is arguably the key to success. The Tyneside Cinema has a long-term strategy of marketing itself based on its independence – unlike many regional art-house cinemas it is not part of a chain. The cinema is located in the only former newsreel cinema still operating as a cinema. It first opened in 1937 as Newcastle News Theatre and remained one of two successful cinemas in the city specialising in newsreels, documentaries and travelogues until the late 1960s when competition from television caused it and its rival, the Tatler, to close (in 1968 and 1969 respectively). The cinema reopened in 1969 with support from the British Film Institute first as the Tyneside Film Theatre, and then under its present name of the Tyneside Cinema. Newcastle's independent cinema has had to find various strategies to improve audience numbers since 1999, when it found itself in trouble with low box office figures. Since then, it has seen a 15% increase, to the point that it is now able to justify an expansion with the addition of a further screen, which should improve its ability to compete in the market. As part of the Europa network, and as a specialist cinema benefiting from BFI support, the Tyneside Cinema has certain responsibilities in terms of education and the screening of European-made films. In recent years, it has become associated with two annual film festivals: the AV Film Festival, a showcase for digital media, and the Northern Lights Film Festival which presents films from across Northern Europe.

Figure 1: Left:
The Empire at the Gate, Newcastle.

Figure 2: Below left:
The Empire at the Gate, Newcastle.

Figure 3: Below:
The Tyneside Film Theatre.
Photograph: Peter Hepplewhite

Figure 4: Above: The Star and Shadow.

Figure 5: Below: The Star and Shadow.

After extensive consultation with its users and its benefactors, the Tyneside Cinema is currently undergoing a major redevelopment, involving the restoration of the Pilgrim Street building to the former glories of the News Theatre, with the addition of more modern facilities to improve access (a lift, new toilets) and, most importantly in terms of its programming potential, a fourth screen. Once building work is complete in 2008, the cinema will boast one large screen (the original News Theatre auditorium), two smaller screens, and a fourth screen in the digital projection facility, the digital lounge. This ties in with an aim to further increase audience numbers by a third again, from 90,000 entries in 2005–06, to 120,000 in 2008–09. This aim is set against a background of cinema attendance in the North East of 6.2 million tickets sold per year – putting into perspective somewhat the share of the market of specialised cinemas (before the move to Gateshead where there is now only one screen, Tyneside Cinema's share represented 1.4% of this figure).

The cinema operates a Friends scheme, and relies heavily on the loyalty of its core audience. Closing the building for 2 years, then, in order to carry out extensive renovations and new building, is a calculated risk. In order to retain as many audience members as possible whilst building work is going on, the Tyneside has moved its operation to the Gateshead Old Town Hall, allowing it to run a reduced programme on just one screen. It will be interesting to monitor the success of this strategy, to observe whether audiences used to the Newcastle city centre venue will venture to the other side of the river, and what they will make of the Gateshead venue which does not have the same proximity to cafés and bars as the Pilgrim Street building. There has been an attempt to provide a sense of continuity, making audiences feel at home with familiar staff and branding, but most particularly with the relocation of the Tyneside Coffee Rooms in the same building as the cinema. It is clear from audience research (questionnaires and focus groups carried out at Newcastle University in February-May 2007, after the closure of the Pilgrim Street building) that the coffee rooms are a key draw for many people, offering a social space linked to cinema-going but not dependent on it. Indeed, for many people, this is the first thing they mention when asked about the Tyneside Cinema.

To give an idea of the range of films shown even with just one screen, the programme for the week 1–8 March 2007 includes: *The Wizard of Oz* (Fleming, 1939); either *Babel* (Iñárritu, 2006) or *The Last King of Scotland* (Macdonald, 2006); *Venus* (Michell, 2006), including a special Silver Screen session; *Pan's Labyrinth* (del Toro, 2006); a Kids' Club screening of *Curious George*

(O'Callaghan, 2006); *Bugsy Malone* (Parker, 1976); *Apocalypto* (Gibson, 2006) and *Little Miss Sunshine* (Dayton and Faris, 2006). The mix includes first runs, repertory films and one-off classics (often targeted to specific audiences, e.g. Silver Screen aimed at older people, or Kids' Club screenings) – screened in English, Spanish, Mayan, and, in the case of the Iñárritu film, a mixture of English, Arabic, Berber, English, French, Japanese and Spanish.

Nonetheless, the Tyneside has had to restrict its operations during its time at Gateshead due to the limited screen space. This may have benefited a more recent arrival on the independent cinema scene in Tyneside, the Star and Shadow Cinema. This community cinema opened for occasional screenings in 2006, and since January 2007 has been running fuller programmes. It is supported by approximately 120 volunteers, with around 20 of these core to the development and programming of the cinema. It is situated in the Ouseburn valley, a part of the city that has benefited from City Council investment through the Ouseburn Trust, charged with responsibility for supporting the regeneration of the area. As a result, it has come to house various different cultural projects (including Seven Stories, the centre for the children's book, as well as of a number of pubs associated with live music, comedy and storytelling).

The cinema was constructed within the shell of the former Tyne Tees Television props department, almost entirely by volunteers. It now boasts an auditorium seating seventy with projection facilities for 16mm, 35mm and digital film, a large rectangular room that can operate as an exhibition space, and a bar area with a film library, an exchange cupboard, and a movable stage, where music and film events take place. In addition to its exhibition activities, the cinema also encourages filmmaking and is in the process of developing its production facilities, including a dark room. The cinema has recently benefited from grants from the Ouseburn Trust and the City Council for the installation of a heating and ventilation system. Unlike the multiplex "spaces of flow", where audience members are "processed" from one queue to the next (for tickets, for the concession stands, for entry into the auditoria), there has been a concerted attempt here to develop this new found space as social space that people are encouraged to use in multiple ways: the bar operates as a film library, a venue for live music, a recycling point, and an exhibition venue.

The Star and Shadow grew out of the collaboration between members of a collective who were based at the Waygood Gallery and who programmed the Side Cinema between 2001 and 2005. This small exhibition site, located close to the

Quayside, belongs to Amber Films, but was leased to this group for the projection of films falling into four main categories: classic and experimental/avant-garde film (Cineside); gay and lesbian film (Other Side); artists' films (A-Side) and political cinema (Radical Side) (*see Figures 3 and 4*). The move to the new premises has given the group greater autonomy over the space within which they operate – their offices and exhibition space are now located within the same building and they are able to operate a bar which provides an important social space for volunteers and audiences, as well as a small income. As a result, they have been able to expand their programme, adding world cinema to their portfolio, with a strong focus on providing films for minority local communities (e.g. Tamils, Bangladeshis, Arab-speaking communities), rather than on world cinema understood as international, non-European or US art-house fare. The volunteer ethos ensures more or less total independence as far as this is possible within the framework of local authority regulations: there is no requirement to make a profit, nor are they tied into the usual patterns of distribution that restrict the programming choices of multiplex and even independent art-house cinemas. This enables a democratic programming policy: volunteers are invited to put on films they would like to see – in particular films that are unlikely to be taken up by the Tyneside Cinema or the multiplexes (although there is a potential overlap with the Metrocentre multi-screen cinema which offers some Bollywood films as well as the more usual blockbusters and Hollywood genre pictures). To offer an example, the current week's programme includes: *Offside* (Jafar Panahi, 2006) an Iranian film about a group of women attempting to infiltrate a men-only football stadium to watch a match, programmed with *Meet Me* (2007) a film made by Newcastle-based asylum seekers; a Renoir double bill of *Une Partie de Campagne* (1936) and *La Grande Illusion* (1937), part of a Poetic Realism season; *Rising Son, The Legend of*, a film following the career of skateboarder Christian Hoisoi; *Dreams of Sparrows* (Hayder Mousa Daffar, 2005), an Iraqi documentary about life in Baghdad post-Saddam; and "Mirrors of Maya", a Maya Deren evening including a screening of *Meshes of the Afternoon* (Deren, 1943) along with experimental dance films from artists based in the North East, and the documentary In the *Mirror of Maya Deren* (Martina Kudlacek, 2001).

Harbord describes the institutionalisation of exhibition sites in Europe into three main categories: "the multiplex cinema, the independent arthouse cinema and the art gallery" – categories which should not be seen as discrete but as possessing permeable boundaries crossed by both films and audiences. She refuses the art-house/multiplex dichotomy, instead arguing that there is a "dynamic structural play" between such sites which is rooted in "the complex formation of cultural fields as historical and spatial entities" (Harbord, 2002: 40). Thus it is still true that "the context of exhibition contributes to the social value of film cultures," which must be seen as "institutionally and spatially [and we could add historically] located" (Harbord, 2002: 39). Such a conceptualisation of exhibition venues would appear to concord with the picture presented above of cinema audiences since 1984, where rising figures for the multiplexes have not necessarily led to a corresponding drop in audiences for independent and specialist cinemas. In addition, when we focus on the picture in Newcastle, we can see that the arrival of the multiplex in the city centre, far from killing off independent cinemas, has in fact been accompanied by the substantial expansion of the Tyneside Cinema. Though the impact of the redevelopment on audiences remains to be seen, the greater flexibility afforded by an extra screen will enable the cinema to broaden their reach. The activities associated with the redevelopment involving local communities (oral history projects, filmmaking work in schools), should also do their bit to raise the cinema's profile with sections of the population who do not identify themselves as belonging to the "cappuccino and carrot cake crowd" associated with art-house cinemas. This has also been a period characterised by the proliferation of "microplex" venues, whose cooperative ethos arguably locates them somewhere beyond the institutional framework posited by Harbord, and although they must inevitably engage with the "dynamic structural play" between the different exhibition sites, they offer something of a return to the "multiplicity of possibilities (of political transformation, of bodily pleasure, of an imbrication of art and life)" that Harbord identifies with cinema in the early twentieth century (Harbord, 2002: 39). This seems like a particularly appropriate way of marking the centenary of cinemas in our town.

Notes

1. See Jancovich and Faire (2003), for an example of how focusing on a specific geographical location (in their case Nottingham) can offer particular insights into the industrial, social and cultural aspects of cinema-going.
2. Manders (1991: 114) refers in particular to Duke Ellington's appearance there in 1958, while a questionnaire respondent remembers seeing Diana Ross there.

References

Allison, D. (2006) 'Multiplex programming in the UK: the economics of homogeneity', *Screen*, 47.1, pp. 81–90.

Anon., The Gate Newcastle – Empire Cinema. Available at: http://www.thegatenewcastle.co.uk/venues/empireCinema.aspx (Accessed: 18 June 2007).

Bourdieu, P. (1984) *Distinction: A Social Critique of the Judgement of Taste*, trans. by R. Nice. Cambridge, Mass.: Harvard University Press.

Doyle, B. (2003) 'The geography of cinemagoing in Great Britain, 1934–1994: a comment', *Historical Journal of Film, Radio and Television*, 23.1, pp. 59–71.

Eyles, A. (1997) 'Exhibition and the cinema-going experience', in R. Murphy (ed.) *The British Cinema Book*. London: BFI, pp. 217–225.

Gomery, D. (1992) *Shared Pleasures: A History of Movie Exhibition in America*. London: BFI.

Hubbard, P. (2003) 'A Good Night Out? Multiplex cinemas as sites of embodied leisure', *Leisure Studies*, 22 (July), pp. 255–272.

Jancovich, M. & Faire, L. with Stubbings, S. (2003) *The Place of the Audience: Cultural Geographies of Film Consumption*. London: BFI.

Kerrigan, F. & Özbilgin, M. (2002) 'Art for the masses or art for the few? Ethical issues in film marketing in the UK', *International Journal of Nonprofit and Voluntary Sector Marketing* 7.2, pp. 195-203.

Manders, F. (1991) *Cinemas of Newcastle: A Comprehensive history of the cinemas of Newcastle upon Tyne*. Newcastle: City of Newcastle upon Tyne, City Libraries and Arts.

Marks, L.U. (2000) *The Skin of the Film: Intercultural cinema, embodiment and the senses*. Durham N.C.: Duke University Press.

(2002) *Touch: Sensuous theory and multisensory media*. Minneapolis: Minnesota University Press.

Sobchack, V. (1992) *The Address of the Eye: A phenomenology of film experience*. Princeton, N.J.: Princeton University Press.

Shaviro, S. (1993) *The Cinematic Body*, Minneapolis: University of Minnesota Press.

UK Box Office Statistics Archive, UK Film Council. Available at: http://www.ukfilmcouncil.org.uk/cinemagoing/archive/?&skip=156 (Accessed: 19 January 2007).

Chapter Seven

From *Launch* to *Shooting Magpies*: Locating the Amber Film Collective

Tobias Hochscherf and James Leggott

The Amber Collective was founded in 1968 by a group of London-based students who moved to the North East with the prime aim of documenting the working-class communities of the region. They were drawn in particular to Newcastle, a city that displayed its rich industrial past not merely by way of bridges and railways, but through its quays, docks and terraces (see Martin, 2002: 159–161).

Amber's arrival coincided with the rise of the regional workshop movement, of which the Collective would become a key player. But whilst other independent groups remain mostly as footnotes in traditional histories of British film-making, Amber is still very much part of the cultural landscape. Over the last forty or so years they have been producing a body of highly regarded, if relatively unknown work, encompassing documentary portraits, community projects, feature films and photographic exhibitions. Given that the majority of their documentary portraits and feature films (which will be the main focus of this chapter) engage, to some degree, with social and political issues, and that Amber has never sought to conceal its socialist impulse, it is hardly surprising that their work has triggered debate, and, in some cases, controversy and even hostility.

Amber are located in a street named the Side that snakes down to historic Quayside, right under the shadow of the Tyne Bridge. The group have been based there since 1977, when they also opened the Side Gallery for international photographic exhibitions. Their distinctly warren-like base also houses a small cinema and a popular Café Bistro. Purchasing this property may have seemed like a perverse decision at a time when other local businesses were moving out of the Quayside area, not least because the City Council seemed intent on running it down as a prelude to demolition. Amber had always been interested in documenting the industries around the river, but their *Quayside* film of 1979 – which captured the decaying streets around the riverside – played no small part in the campaign to save this threatened part of the city, which ultimately led to the most historic buildings being granted listed status.

Today, the Quayside is thriving and Amber's own reputation for innovation and commitment to the region remains as secure as ever. As one of the few remaining practitioners of the workshop movement that flourished in the 1970s and 1980s, they enjoy a unique position within British film culture. But it is a precarious one too, for despite their admirable engagement with the possibilities of digital technologies, they face continual problems in getting their work distributed and exhibited. Amber had been one of the key players in the development of the

ACTT workshop agreement of 1984, which gave structural and financial stability to those working outside the film and broadcasting mainstream. The blossoming of the movement during the 1980s was partly the result of the relatively generous funding given to independent film-makers by Channel Four television; the channel had been given a remit to promote independent and minority voices at a time when public film funding had been curtailed by the Conservative government brought to power in 1979. That an oppositional movement should thrive as the direct result of Thatcherite policy is a peculiar irony, particularly as the intervening years have been increasingly difficult for maverick operations like Amber. The problems of visibility are highlighted by the respective fates of their feature films *Dream On* (1990) and *Like Father* (2001). *Dream On* was shown on Channel Four following a seven-week run at the Newcastle Odeon, whereas *Like Father*, partly funded by the BBC, was relegated to one of their digital channels. The threat of escalating marginality has prompted Amber to consider new strategies for distribution. Their most recent project, *Shooting Magpies* (2005) – given some developmental funding by Channel Four – was shot on digital video (DV) and Amber toyed with the possibilities of an online premiere. Indeed, if Amber's work has been increasingly difficult to see in theatres or on television, their back catalogue is more accessible than ever since their films have been made available on the internet (primarily to academic institutions) for download and streaming. Mindful of their legacy, perhaps, the Collective has also embarked on a process of re-mastering their feature films for DVD release. Their first reissue, of one of their most celebrated films, *In Fading Light* (1989), was packaged with new documentaries about Amber's involvement with the shipbuilding and fishing industries of Tyneside, and reminiscences about the making of the film by those involved. These new films, alongside a short booklet on the history of the Collective, were supported by a Heritage Lottery pilot project looking at ways to document Amber's work in the North-East.

Given the diversity and scope of Amber's output, but also its thematic and aesthetic coherence, it is disappointing that they have so far escaped substantial critical attention. One might argue that the limited academic interest in Amber is indicative of a bias towards popular genre film-making in the identification and appraisal of national cinematic traditions. In other words, Amber does not make a straightforward fit into the established categories of British film and television culture. On the one hand, their place in the established canon of British realist cinema is problematised by their unorthodox working methods. There is no mention, for example, of Amber in Samantha Lay's overview (2002) of the paths taken by British social realism since the documentary films of the 1930s. On the other hand, this very dedication to the cause of realism renders their work distasteful (and even archaic) to those who align 'independence' purely with modernist or avant-garde strategies. In fact, in contrast with European traditions of art cinema, and despite its own academic roots and early forays into experimental territory (such as *A Film*, 1969), Amber have never promoted elitist or intellectual notions of art. While it is debatable as to whether their films offer a romanticised and nostalgic picture of working class life, their realist approach has made their films theoretically accessible to a broad audience.

Amber and Realist Practice

Any detailed discussion of Amber's developing artistic strategies would therefore need to consider how their work brings together various traditions of documentary and feature film, namely, the independent workshop movement, currents of realist practice and even auteurist procedures. Amber's relation to documentary traditions that straddle national boundaries also demands scrutiny. It is our intention here, however, to narrow the focus to a consideration of how Amber's work can be connected to a tradition of British social realist cinema perhaps best exemplified by the 1930s documentary movement (commonly associated with Grierson and Jennings), the films of the so-called New Wave, and the work of veterans such as Ken Loach. Amber's feature films can be read as a kind of commentary on this tradition, in that their films acknowledge, address and even dramatise some of the perceived problems with realist practice. Recurring debates around such issues as authenticity, romanticism and, in particular, intervention and adaptation, are woven into the very fabric of the films themselves, thus circumventing, some of the alleged pitfalls of this kind of film-making.

A key concern for Amber has been to document the voices of the marginalised. This tallies with the general tendency within social realist cinema towards representational extension. Amber deliberately shifted their initial focus away from (post-)industrial Tyneside towards more peripheral communities, such as those involved in the declining fishing industry of North Shields, and most recently, the former coalfields of East Durham. This emphasis upon rural environments – as seen for example in Eden Valley (1994), which is set amidst a harness-racing community – is relatively unprecedented in British realist cinema. Similarly, if the realist tradition, from the likes of *Saturday Night* and *Sunday Morning* (1960) through to *Nil By Mouth* (1997) has largely been concerned, with the odd exception, with masculine experience, Amber has worked to redress this gender imbalance through narratives told from a female perspective, such as *Dream On* and *The Scar* (1997). Indeed, in its telling of the experiences of women who had organised support for the miners during their strikes against pit closures, *The Scar* offers a somewhat different view of the unsuccessful industrial action of the 1980s – and the resultant social and economic changes – than such predominantly male-centred films as *Billy Elliot* (2001) and *Brassed Off* (1996). Whilst the latter film does feature campaigning women, they are merely part of the mise-en-scène rather than a central concern of the film, a lack which *The Scar* seeks to address.

However, an examination of Amber's work is not only worthwhile in terms of representation but also with regard to their unorthodox modes of production. Typically, their projects take shape organically, each work connecting back to its antecedents, and then sowing the seeds for future ventures. For example, the making of *Seacoal* (1985) brought the creative team into contact with the world of trotting horses, which then became the focus for *Eden Valley* roughly ten years later. *Eden Valley* then led Amber to County Durham, which has become the setting for their subsequent feature films. All of these are concerned with the social, economic and physical impact of the decline of the coalfields. The roots of all these films are the 'real' experiences of people in these specific places; for example, with *Like Father*, once the team had decided to focus upon male experience, the process began with video interviews, drama groups and video camera workshops with boys and men within differing age ranges, from which they found their characters and stories, as well as their principal actors.

The dedication of the Amber to the telling of stories from deep within their chosen communities produces undoubtedly authentic material. Their devotion to both the cause of realism and the communities themselves is clear, for example, from their involvement in the purchase of a pub – which was used in *Dream On* – and of a decommissioned boat which they operated in North Shields harbour over the course of three years, and which became one of the key settings for *In Fading Light*.

But despite such noble intentions, Amber can not utterly free themselves from one of the accusations that has been frequently levelled at practitioners of social realism, namely, that the film-makers' perspective can only ever be that of the outsider. In the case of the so-called British New Wave of the 1950s and 1960s, for example, Andrew Higson (1984) has argued that the metropolitan, middle-class viewpoint of the film-makers is ultimately inscribed within their corpus. To their credit, though, Amber have acknowledged this potential problem, conceding that one of their most famous early documentaries, *Launch* (1973) which depicts the departure of a ship from a yard in Wallsend – is open to charges of romanticism (*see Figure 1*). There is certainly a nostalgic impulse at work in recent films such as *Like Father* and *The Scar*, which promote depleted coalfield areas as places of extraordinary beauty, just as there is a celebration of manual toil throughout Amber's oeuvre that could feasibly be described as romantic. However, the team have argued that they are merely offering a reflection of how their subjects perceive their own environment and work. At the end of *Amber: A Short History*, the booklet produced by the Collective in 2006, there is a quotation from R.G. Collingwood's *The Principles of Art* (1938) that expresses a similar sentiment: "the artist must talk of the problems of the community he serves, not his own, because they are interested in their own dilemmas, not those of the artist" (cited in Amber, 2006). This statement also appeared for some time on an introductory section on Amber's website (which was redeveloped in Spring 2007), but it was followed by a recognition that the reality of the work is invariably more complex, and that members of the Amber team have "frequently found metaphors for their own struggles in the documents they have created" (Amber 2007).

This is a telling admission, and it perhaps points towards what makes the Amber films so rich and unusual within contemporary British social realist cinema, that is, the manner in which the experiences of both participants and creative team are embedded within the text. It is apt, given the nature of the creative process, and the close involvement of the creative team within the communities they depict, that so many Amber films dramatise and question processes of intervention. Unlike the films, say, of Ken Loach, where powerless characters are propelled towards tragedy by forces beyond their control, the Amber films convey a greater optimism about the individual's capacity to shape his or her future. However, the life changes that occur within Amber narratives often arrive through some kind of intervening character.

One example of this mediator figure is the character of Peggy in *Dream On*, an Irish woman who comes to visit her son, Bert, who runs a pub in North Shields. *Dream On* centres upon three female characters, each beset by problems ranging from an abusive relationship to an eating disorder, who come together for a weekly darts match in their local pub. It is the benevolent interference of the Peggy character that brings the women to realise their own capacity for change; having

Figure 1: Left: Launch.
Photograph: Amber films.

Figure 2: Below: T. Dan Smith.
Photograph: Amber films.

Figure 3: Above: In Fading Light Crew Shot. Photograph: Peter Fryer.

Figure 4: Below: Shooting Magpies. Photograph: Amber films.

achieved this aim, to a degree, she leaves the community at the end of the film, at the moment when the women are celebrating the victory of their darts team.

The stories that formed the narrative of *Dream On* were developed from a women's writing workshop led by a member of the Collective. Consequently, it is tempting to see the mysterious Peggy character, and her impact on the community, as a surrogate for this real-life mediator figure, and, by extension, for the film-makers themselves. Indeed, the place where the women come to play darts, and escape their traumatic home lives, happens to be the pub which the Collective themselves had bought; the characters, and the real-life stories behind them, find refuge in a space literally created by the film-makers.

This may sound like self-aggrandising on behalf of the Collective, keen to emphasise how their projects have transformed the lives of their participants. Furthermore, Amber has also helped to promote the careers of local writers and actors (they claim to have given Robson Green his first screen experience). But this self-referential foregrounding of the developmental process can also be deemed to be essentially honest, with the film-makers openly acknowledging their mediating role, as they also tend to do in their documentary features. Their 1983 film *Byker*, for example, is a document of the communities of the East End of Newcastle, through the eyes of the photographer Sirkka Konttinen, one of the founder members of the Collective who had actually been living in the area, amongst her subjects, since moving to Tyneside in the 1960s. The documentary process is exposed further in a profile of the disgraced council leader *T. Dan Smith* (1987). This fascinating film stands as a reminder that any discussion of Amber's self-reflexive strategies ought not be restricted to their fictional work. In fact, the provocatively anti-realist *T. Dan Smith* can be understood as a kind of conceptual documentary, combing interviews with Smith and footage of the film-makers discussing how they should shape their material and what kind of stance they should take on their subject. Described by Martin Hunt as "one of the most innovative and challenging documentaries to have been broadcast in Britain" (Hunt, 2007a), the film not only offers an interrogation of editorial procedures, but opens a space for the viewer to reach their own verdict on the charismatic politician, best remembered now for his part in the Poulson Scandal of the late 1960s. Although unique in terms of form and content, *T. Dan Smith*, as Martin Hunt argues, "shares with Amber's other work a respect for its audience and a political stance that is interrogative without being didactic" (Hunt, 2007b) (*see Figure 2*).

There are frequent reminders, across Amber's work, of the limits of editorial or creative interference. In *The Filleting Machine* (1981) one of Amber's earliest explorations of the dramatic format, a North Shields quay worker compares his life of manual labour to that of a white-collar worker: "that's what you call work... there's not a writer born can put that doon". Ironically, this part is played by the esteemed playwright Tom Hadaway, who happened also to write the script, drawing upon his own experiences of the fishing industry. There's an equivalent acknowledgement of dramatic artifice in *Dream On*, when, after an evening of melodramatic revelations and confrontations, a character comments that she had "a strange night: like being in a play" (*see Figure 3*).

Amber in the Twenty-first Century:
Like Father and *Shooting Magpies*

Since the mid-1990s, Amber have focussed their attention primarily on the landscapes and communities of the former coalfield areas of East Durham. The resulting documentaries, photographic exhibitions and feature films engage with the traumatic aftermath of the final coalfield closures, and the awkward shift to a post-industrial age. Taken together, the trilogy of feature films produced over the past decade, represent an attempt to explore the past, present and future of the region, from differing perspectives of age and gender. *The Scar* deals with the impact – both psychological and physical – of the failure of the miners' strike, and does so from a mostly female perspective. The centrepiece of the Durham triptych, *Like Father* (2001), is perhaps the most schematic of the films, exploring the impact of a coastal regeneration scheme and the necessary demolition of allotment gardens upon three male generations of one family. *Shooting Magpies* is arguably less overtly political, with its story of a young mother who struggles to rescue her partner from heroin addiction; nevertheless, it diagnoses the despondency of an entire generation without hope of employment (*see Figure 4*).

Amber's general approach to story-telling remains fairly consistent across these films. Few professional actors are cast, and they appear mostly in the role of authority figures, although the central character of *The Scar* was played by a professional actress, and two of the main roles in *Shooting Magpies* are played by actors who had appeared in previous Amber productions. Otherwise, the participants tend to play parts based upon their own experiences. The fictional narrative of *Shooting Magpies* evolved out of the stories told to the group by the two people who would eventually be given the lead roles. Emma Dowson had been involved in an Amber project about the experiences of teenage mothers, and Barry Gough, a youth worker, had assisted the group with a youth fundraising project, and also been featured as part of the Coalfield Stories project of photographing the region.

As dramatisations of Amber's creative processes, the two most recent feature films are particularly interesting, but they can also be read as a commentary upon key tropes of the contemporary realist film. The emphasis in *Like Father* upon the plight of men and boys in post-industrial northern communities is in many ways typical of British social realist cinema. In a similar – yet less comical – fashion to successful films such as *The Full Monty* (1997) and *Billy Elliot*, it raises questions about the empowering possibilities of strategies of performance. Inevitably, *Like Father* invites comparison with the latter film, which dwells upon changing gender roles by way of a story about a young boy who escapes the tensions of the 1984 miners' strike to become a star of the ballet world. The central characters of both films share not only a surname and a landscape (*Billy Elliot* was also filmed in East Durham), but a dedication to processes of regeneration. John Hill notes how "in a loose allegory of the transition from a manufacturing to a service-based economy, Billy [Elliot] becomes an emblem of economic rejuvenation through participation in the 'creative industries'" (Hill, 2004: 108). In *Like Father*, this impulse is personified by the central character of Joe Elliot, yet another of Amber's surrogate figures, here faced with the problem of how to represent a weakened community through music. Joe is an ex-miner, now working as a teacher and musician and running his own booking agency ('Class Acts') for entertainers. This acceptance of the necessity for adaptation in the post-industrial climate contrasts with the aggressive response of his father, Arthur, to the coastal regeneration scheme that requires the removal of his allotment and pigeon-loft. There is familial tension when Arthur hears that Joe has been commissioned to write a brass band suite to commemorate the opening of the scheme. Joe finds inspiration for his three-part musical score – based around the idea of the past, present and future – from the landscape and his recollection of the 'rhythms of the pits'. The resulting work is posited as celebratory, not least because it is emblematic of the film's own narrative strategy, and this sense of optimism only exacerbated by the knowledge that the actor playing the part of Joe happened to write the musical score for the film itself.

However, the film acknowledges some problems with the idea of performance and creativity as a regenerative strategy for ex-mining communities to overcome disenfranchisement. Joe progresses well with his musical score, but the pressures of work cause him to lose contact with his troubled young son Michael. The film concludes with a family reunion of sorts, and a suggestion that Joe has chosen to abandon his musical commission – which could have launched alucrative career – out of a sense of family loyalty.

Amber's subsequent feature film, *Shooting Magpies* – which forms the third part of their County Durham trilogy – offers a similar lament for the generations raised in the post-industrial era. At the same time, the film marks both an evolution and consolidation of Amber's creative strategy, and in doing so, raises questions not only about the prospects for threatened communities, but about the future of realist film practice and consumption. As indicated, *Shooting Magpies* adopts the customary Amber strategy of developing a narrative out of the stories told by local residents. In a kind of self-assessment of the Collective's own impact on their subjects, the film poses doubts about the motivations and effectiveness of its main mediating figure, Barry, a former social worker who acts as mentor to a young woman struggling with her 'smackhead' boyfriend. The ethical problems raised by the personal involvement of the film-makers in the lives of their subjects are acknowledged by a member of the Collective on the film's accompanying documentary. The film's evocation of a pernicious drug culture is in some regards reminiscent of Ken Loach's Glasgow-set films of recent years. Both *My Name is Joe* (1997) and *Sweet Sixteen* (2001) describe how an effort by a sympathetic character to 'save' a heroin addict generates some very difficult choices, and ultimately a violent encounter with gangland leaders.

Whilst *Shooting Magpies* builds upon Amber's longstanding tradition of interaction, the decision to shoot for the first time using digital video had some interesting implications for the production process and ultimately the aesthetics of the film. Amber had used video for their documentary projects in the past, but the deployment of lightweight, inexpensive DV cameras for filming a feature – in part, a budgetary necessity – had various benefits, as discussed by the Amber team in the 62-minute film, *The Making of Shooting Magpies*, which is a additional feature of the film's DVD release. As far of the participants were concerned, the considerably smaller DV equipment allowed for reduced set-up times, almost unlimited and unobtrusive access to people's homes, and a greater mobility in general. However, as the film-makers acknowledge, the use of DV also results in some aesthetic idiosyncrasies such as the loss of lighting as a storytelling tool and also a certain degree of saturation; compositions in *Shooting Magpies* featuring green grass or blue skies look particularly vivid.

Still, for the film-makers, the adoption of DV would seem to mark a change in visual style. If their early documentaries are characterised by a succession of numerous static medium shots, the fluid, responsive camerawork of *Shooting Magpies* is perhaps more reminiscent of the Direct Cinema film-makers of the 1950s and 1960s, such as D.A. Pennebaker, who invented his own miniature cameras to grant the audience closer involvement to the subject. In terms of fictional film-making, however, the decision to rely on location-shooting and natural light brings to mind the visual approaches of those who chose to follow the infamous Dogme 95 "Vow of Chastity". The use of DV also meant that the creative team could re-shape the film in-house by way of digital editing so as to best serve their story. It would seem that a non-linear approach was at one point tried and rejected, although an element of dislocation remains through a handful of dream-like, initially enigmatic sequences that act as flashbacks or flashforwards.

Perhaps more significant, however, is the effect of using a visual style that for many spectators may be reminiscent of certain television formats. Although the use of DV cameras can partly be understood as a continuation of the Direct Cinema impulse to bridge the gap between audience and subject, this relationship is challenged in *Shooting Magpies* by the use of on-screen interviews, and also by moments where the characters turn directly to speak to the camera. Just as the contrivances of the narrative as acknowledged in other films such as *Dream On*, here too the character of Barry responds to a surprising encounter with an address to the audience: "It's not everyday you get your money back off a smackhead, is it?". These instances of direct address may well be intended to position the viewer as confidante and thus to heighten involvement, but they could also be experienced as moments of rupture within the otherwise conventionally "realist" narrative. Furthermore, they function as reminders of how the film developed out of documentary projects involving the main actors; the main players were chosen for their abilities as story-tellers as much as for their capacity to re-imagine events from their real lives within a fictional framework. The resulting ambiguity is particularly notable in a sequence which incorporates footage of the Queen visiting East Durham. Whilst this section offers, in a similar way to the royal visit shown in the earlier film *Launch*, a visible contrast between the high-society grandeur of the monarchy and the alarming living conditions of Her Majesty's subjects in some areas of the post-industrial North East, the audience is left with some doubt as to whether the event is real or staged; an unease the film itself does little to dispel in the way it playfully mixes and bends generic expectations.

The blurring of the distinctions between drama and documentary is hardly new in Amber's work, but the adoption of self-reflexive strategies in conjunction with the use of digital video produces a realist effect that bears some similarity – in terms of its address to the viewer, if not its intent – with indexical reproductions of actual events in contemporary "reality" formats on television. A characteristic of contemporary documentary programming in Britain and beyond is the incorporation of some kind of authentic experience within a transparently artificial framework, as typified by formats such as *Faking It*, *Wife Swap*, or even *Big Brother*. This is not to suggest that *Shooting Magpies* represents Amber's commentary on reality television, yet the film certainly calls attention to the manner in which programme formats can balance their direct engagement with "reality" with the reassurance of distance (see Fetveit, 2003: 551). To condemn *Shooting Magpies*, like the majority of Amber's hybridised work, for its confusion of narrative codes – its combination of moments of verisimilitude with markers of artificiality – is to underestimate the literacy of audience who are willing to respond to the emotional and social accuracy of material they comprehend as staged. For Amber, accessibility has to be prioritised over intellectual experiment, but this is not to suggest that films such as *Shooting Magpies* are straightforward, or incapable of multiple readings. Their best work not only engages with locally relevant stories, but opens up questions of realist practice, technical approaches and artistic self-expression.

Further questions about the intricate relationship between Amber, their subjects and their audience are raised by the manner in which *Shooting Magpies* has been packaged for a domestic audience. Whilst the film has been shown in venues across the North East of England, and at some international festivals, a significant number of people are likely to encounter the film on DVD, which offers an intriguingly multifaceted and interactive viewing experience, reminding the viewer simultaneously of the film's claim to authenticity and its constructed status. The film is accompanied by the aforementioned documentary in which the creative team describe the genesis, production and aftermath of the film. There are also excerpts from documentaries about the two main characters, and a slideshow of photographic images from the Coalfield Stories project. Of course, it is not unusual for movies to be packaged with "bonus" features, but the extensive contextualising material here – which has a narrative (and documentary) interest of its own – is a reminder that the finished film is only part of the story.

Locating Amber's centre of operations in the heart of Newcastle can be a challenge to the visitor, who must negotiate a dimly-lit alley and some particularly hazardous stairs. But if Amber is hard to find – quite literally – one senses that this is comfortable for them. Their status as non-conformists, or, indeed, the industry "outsider", allows them to pursue their evolving strategies of community involvement and formal experimentation free, by and large, from commercial restraints – as well as providing a vantage-point from which to query some of the dominant tropes of social realist cinema and practice. Their own individual way of approaching new themes and willingness to seek new opportunities of funding, production and distribution has certainly helped to sustain their status among Britain's leading independent filmmakers. Yet what renders their work so unique, and worthy of attention, is the way in which the experiences of the film-makers, like those of their subjects, are far from hidden. The manner in which real lives are embedded within their films permits a celebration of both the creative team and the communities to which they are committed.

References

Amber (2006) *Amber: A Short History.* A brochure produced by the Collective for inclusion in DVD releases.

Amber (2007). 'Amber Online'. Available at: http://www.amber-online.com/html/amber_history.html (Accessed: 10 March 2007).

Fetveit, A. (2003) 'Reality TV in the Digital Era: A Paradox in Visual Culture?', in R. Allen & A Hill (eds) *The Television Studies Reader.* London: Routledge, pp. 543-556.

Higson, A. (1984) 'Space, place, spectacle: Landscape and townscape in the "kitchen sink" film', *Screen,* 25 (4-5), pp. 2–21.

Hill, J. (2004) 'A Working-Class Hero Is Something to Be? Changing Representations of Class and Masculinity in British Cinema', in P. Powrie *et al.* (eds) *The Trouble with Men: Masculinities in European and Hollywood Cinema.* London: Wallflower. pp. 100–109.

Hunt, M. (2007a). 'T. Dan Smith'. Available at: http://www.screenonline.org.uk/film/id/503909/index.html. (Accessed: 10 March 2007).

Hunt, M. (2007b) 'Amber Collective (1969–)'. Available at: http://www.screenonline.org.uk/people/id/502352/index.html. (Accessed: 10 March 2007).

Lay, S. (2002) *British Social Realism: From Documentary to Brit Grit.* London: Wallflower.

Martin, M. (2002) 'Documentary Poet', Murray Martin interviewed by Huw Beynon, in S. Rowbotham & H. Beynon (eds.) *Looking at Class: Film, Television and the Working Class in Britain.* London: Rivers Oram, pp.159–172.

Chapter Eight

**Toon on the TV:
The Televisual Rebranding of Newcastle,
from *Our Friends in the North* (1996)
to *55° North* (2004–05)**

David Martin-Jones

This chapter explores the changing representation of Newcastle on television, from *Our Friends in the North* (1996) to *55° North* (2004–05). Their differing depictions of the city of Newcastle are seen to mirror shifting national attitudes towards Newcastle as it underwent a process of gentrification in the 1990s, a phenomenon that is discussed in detail in their collection by Paul Usherwood and Chris Wharton. This rebranding saw the city's image change from that of a (supposed) industrial wasteland to a vibrant centre of entertainment and culture. The differing aesthetic styles and narrative themes of the two series are contrasted, as are the broadcasting agendas that shaped them and the shifting national contexts they negotiate. In this way a picture emerges of the extent to which the city's economic, cultural and institutional rejuvenation has been paralleled by its televisual makeover, as Newcastle was rebranded as a vital part of post-industrial England.

When *Match of the Day* returned to BBC1 in 2004 the revamped title sequence firmly established the nationally recognisable face of recently rebranded Newcastle. The football stadia of England's major premiership teams are introduced through close-ups of computer generated team badges, which rise up from the pitch to hover above their respective stadiums. Reflecting the Premiership's financial contribution to England's economy, these badges appear like supernatural corporate logos radiating the light of economic benefit to the surrounding cities. Yet when Newcastle's St James' Park appears something slightly different happens. The badge is initially seen dominating the sky above the ground as per all the other clubs, but then an unusual cut is deployed to a long shot which re-establishes the location of the badge/ground in the middle distance. In this shot the city becomes a backdrop to the distinctive span of the Millennium Bridge and the trendy bars of the Quayside alongside the Tyne. Considering the predominance of the London clubs in the Premiership this is a startling acknowledgement of Newcastle's rejuvenated status, and indeed, its national prominence.

In fact, this blatant advert for Newcastle as a thriving city summed up by the image of the Millennium Bridge and the Quayside is not unusual for the BBC. In February 2003 the BALTIC Centre for the Contemporary Arts in Gateshead – a converted flour mill linked to the Quayside's major concentration of pubs and clubs by the Millennium Bridge – hosted a televised *Newsnight* in which Tony Blair was quizzed by Jeremy Paxman on the war in Iraq. In July 2004, *Top of the Pops* used Baltic Square as the venue for its first ever outdoor show in its forty year history. Finally, in September 2004, returning double Olympic Gold Medallist

Kelly Holmes triumphed in a televised Great North Mile over a route that included the Millennium Bridge and a final straight provided by the Quayside. In BBC coverage in the noughties, then, this gentrified riverside area of Newcastle has increasingly come to represent the post-industrial wealth of the North East.

It is not only the BBC that uses the image of the BALTIC, Millennium Bridge and Quayside to represent Newcastle in this way. The Great North Eastern Railway company (GNER) now publicise Newcastle as one of the six top city destinations worth visiting along their route, along with London, Leeds, Glasgow, York and Edinburgh. Their advertising states:

> Once much-maligned as an industrial backwater, Newcastle and Gateshead – linked by the stunning white arch of the Millennium Bridge – have swapped coal for culture and emerged as a major centre for the arts. The once-derelict Quayside is now home to the North's leading gallery, BALTIC, and The Sage Gateshead, whose sleek aluminium curves house a premier music venue. Buzzing bars and clubs provide entertainment into the small hours ... (GNER website)

GNER's rail ticket packaging also establishes Anthony Gormley's distinctive Angel of the North statue as one of three key landmarks that express their rail network's coverage of the North East, the other two being the London Eye and the Forth Rail Bridge in Edinburgh. Finally, the city's iconic architectural landmarks have also featured prominently in recent films shot in Newcastle, such as *The One and Only* (2002) and *Goal!* (2005). Here the gentrified aspect of post-industrial Newcastle is introduced to central characters visiting from Africa and North America respectively, as this nationally recognisable image of Newcastle is increasingly turned outwards to global markets.

In short, a certain image of the newly rejuvenated Newcastle has recently become nationally, if not internationally, recognisable. This is due to the recurring use of a selective image of Newcastle constructed of the post-industrial pleasure area of the Quayside, the iconic symbol of wealth that is the £22m Millennium Bridge (funded by the Millennium Commission and the European Regional Development Fund), and the symbols of Newcastle's renewed cultural vibrancy – the £46m BALTIC Centre, the Angel of the North and the distinctive £70m Sage Gateshead concert hall, two structures that Paul Usherwood describes in this volume as the "brand" and the "symbol" of rebranded Newcastle. As I shall examine in the remainder of this piece, this is an extremely recent image that replaces that of Newcastle the "industrial backwater" still present in *Our Friends*. In the mainstream crime drama *55° North*, the BBC adds depth to this new image, constantly re-using the same city spaces as locations that re-emphasise the national rebranding of Newcastle as a vibrant city. In this process the series also equates Newcastle with London, England's only global city, suggesting that after London rejuvenated in the 1980s and 1990s the wealth it created spread northwards, the Quayside being evidence that it has now reached Newcastle.

I begin with *Our Friends in the North*. In this serial the well established "industrial backwater" stereotype still existed, although the first indications of the gentrification that was to come were also evident. I then focus in more depth on *55° North*, drawing out the differences between the two. Although there have been a number of other televisual representations of Newcastle in the 1990s and 2000s – everything from *Byker Grove* (1989–) to *Spender* (1991–93) – the two BBC productions in question provide a contrast that illuminates the role of television in revamping the image of certain areas of post-industrial England from – as Chris Wharton has it in his collection – work to consumption.

Our Friends in the North

Our Friends has already received critical attention as a stand-out work of contemporary television drama. For instance it was the subject of one of the four flagship volumes of the BFI's TV Classics range published in 2005, alongside *Buffy*, *Doctor Who* and *The Office*. Thus, although *Our Friends* is an extremely useful series to examine, due to this body of existing literature I will focus on the way it represents Newcastle, and explore it in this respect as a predecessor to *55° North*.

Our Friends is a nine part serial charting the lives of four friends from Newcastle from 1964–1995. They are Nicky (Christopher Eccleston), Geordie (Daniel Craig), Tosker (Mark Strong), and Mary (Gina McKee). Their interlocking lives are used to gain access to the changing political landscape of Britain during the thirty years in question. Each episode is set during a turbulent year, most of which contained a general election. Nicky is an idealistic young man in the 1960s who becomes involved with the labour party, is disillusioned over internal corruption, becomes an anarchist, returns to the Labour party in the 1970s, develops into a professional photographer in the 1980s, and eventually emigrates to Italy. Nicky's friend Geordie leaves Newcastle for London in the 1960s, becomes a gangster in Soho, is imprisoned and ruined by his boss, lives on the streets during the 1980s, and finally returns to Newcastle in the 1990s. Geordie's friend Tosker transforms from disillusioned industrial labourer in the 1970s to a self-made low Tory in the 1980s. Most importantly of all, Mary, who is initially Nicky's girlfriend, marries Tosker and starts a family, later breaks with Tosker and becomes Nicky's wife, and finally, a single mother, is elected as a Labour MP in the 1990s.

Our Friends had a long and complex development process. The fact that it made it to television screens was due to the dedication of writer Peter Flannery and producer Michael Wearing, over fifteen years of pre-production wranglings with various Heads of BBC2 (Eaton, 2005: 10–25). It is often considered worthy of comment as it was so different from most mainstream scheduling in Britain during the 1990s. As Robin Nelson (1997) made clear only one year after its release, *Our Friends* emerged at a time of increasing multi-channel television (be it from cable or satellite sources), when programmes were increasingly forced to compete in a global marketplace. The shift in focus from television addressing national audiences by investigating contemporary political concerns in serial format to transnationally appealing soaps, cop series and apparently apolitical and ahistorical genres like the period drama; seemingly left little room for social realist, regionally set, nationally specific epic serials like *Our Friends* (Nelson, 1997: 240 and Cooke, 2003: 170–74). In the context of ratings wars and public debate over the dumbing-down of TV content, a big budget, single authored serial was anomalous. In content it was more evocative of predecessors like *Boys from the Black Stuff* (1982) (also produced by Wearing) than more popular contemporary shows like *Heartbeat* (1992–). Thus its £7m budget (huge at that time) was an achievement in itself, as was its average audience of 4.6m, and indeed, its BAFTA award for Best Drama Serial in 1997 (Cooke, 2003: 172).

Yet, whilst the serial's progressive credentials are often extolled in this way, what of its representation of Newcastle? The serial's evocation of the "North" through Newcastle is rarely commented on, as though its social realist aesthetic gains credibility simply from being set in Newcastle, regardless of how Newcastle is selectively rendered by the programme, or indeed, of how representative Newcastle is of the North. To put this into perspective one only has to consider how different the serial might have been had it been set in Durham or York, to see how difficult this conflation of the North is with Newcastle. Although it is concerns specific to Newcastle's history as a city that determine how Newcastle is depicted, despite this, *Our Friends* renders Newcastle in line with previously defining stereotypes of the city as an industrial wasteland.

Our Friends' illustrates the struggle that beset Newcastle as it began a process of massive re-housing in the 1960s under local Labour councillor T. Dan Smith. Smith is fictionalised in the serial as one Austin Donohue. Smith's high rise projects were undermined by shoddy materials and working practices, making many of them ultimately unfit for habitation. This was itself the result of local government corruption and bribery involving Smith's favoured construction firm, John Poulson's Open Systems Building (Eaton: 40). Much of the serial is bound up with the narrative of the Willow Lane Flats built by Donohue, including Nicky's initial involvement in the project as Donohue's assistant, Tosker and Mary's experiences living in the deteriorating flats during the 1960s, Nicky's martyr-like inhabitation of them during the 1970s (along with Geordie, drug dealing from a flat down the hall), Nicky's political quest to have them torn down, and his photographing of their eventual destruction. This continuous strand of the story across the decades creates the sense that Newcastle has ultimately failed to rejuvenate in that time. In the image of the Willow Lane Flats in rubble in episode six, Smith's vision of the city as a "Brasilia of the North" on a par with Milan or Manhattan (bbc.co.uk, 2003: "Inside-Out"), is seen to have completely failed. Indeed, the major events that follow in the final three episodes include the miner's strikes of the 1980s, Tosker's opportunistic scheme of providing mortgages to council tenants hoping to buy their own houses, and the increasing lawlessness of Newcastle's unemployed youth, thus further emphasising the "failed" nature of the struggle to rejuvenate the North in Newcastle.

In the final episode set in 1995, however, the notion of a Newcastle as an "industrial backwater" is questioned, and the serial ends with the suggestion that better times are to come. The closing sequence concerns Nicky and Mary's last minute realisation that their perpetually on-off relationship is worth salvaging. As Nicky rushes to catch Mary's car he runs through a changing landscape. Leaving his parents' nineteenth century terrace behind, Nicky puffs his way past the dilapidated fences and garages of the increasingly forgotten industrial Newcastle, finally catching Mary with the Byker Wall strategically placed behind him. The reverse shot, showing Mary from Nicky's point of view, reveals her face framed by the Tyne before the Millennium Bridge, with the pre-renovation Baltic and Newcastle's other distinctive bridges in silhouette. When Nicky proposes to Mary that they try again, she replies with a positive "Why not?" The different frames that the city provides for each character suggest that Newcastle in 1996 is in transition from a period of "failed" social housing schemes (Nicky and the Byker Wall), to a new, apparently brighter future (New Labour Mary and the Quayside).

Moreover, pivotal to this final episode is Tosker's gala opening of his latest project, a floating nightclub on board a docked yacht moored to the Tyne. This is in actual fact a real nightclub, the Tuxedo Princess, moored under the Tyne Bridge within easy staggering distance of the Millennium Bridge. The nightclub opening again hints at the future rejuvenation of this part of the city, Tosker's happy family playing on deck being one of the final images of the city in the serial. Newcastle is thriving, it would seem, due to a combination of dedicated community oriented politics (Mary) and entrepreneurial zeal (Tosker). Although their marriage could not survive in the 1960s, their qualities are now apparently the ideal recipe for a rejuvenation of Newcastle – much as it has seen in the 1990s, and particularly under New Labour – as opposed to all the "failed" attempts by both Labour and the Conservative governments in the preceding thirty years. It is exactly this recipe that would see the Millennium Bridge come to supersede the Tyne Bridge as the quintessential symbol of Newcastle.

55° North

In contrast to the obvious niche appeal of BBC2's *Our Friends*, *55° North* is a prime-time crime drama, produced by Zenith North for BBC Scotland. It began in July 2004, with six 60 minutes episodes on BBC1, at 9pm on Tuesday nights. It ran for two series with an average audience of around 5.7m for the first series, and 4.3m (barb website) for the second. This ran for eight episodes on BBC1, Sunday nights at 8pm, in 2005. At its peak *55° North* outstripped *Our Friends*, and even as its popularity waned during the second series it still pulled in a comparable audience. This is undoubtedly due to the broader appeal of its format.

55° North is an ensemble drama that revolves around protagonist Detective Sergeant Nicky Cole (Don Gilet), a "fish out of water" black London policeman transferred to Newcastle. Nicky is accompanied by his nephew, Matty, and his uncle Errol (George Harris). Nicky is given the unpopular night shift but performs his job well, getting to know the city of Newcastle in the process. He is soon romantically involved with Crown Prosecution Service lawyer Claire Maxwell (Dervla Kirwan).

55° North is a post-modern genre hybrid that appeals to a broad audience by mingling the crime drama with what Richard Sparks (1992) has identified as a soap opera styled focus on the family, juvenile crime, domestic and other social problems (128–29). This is evident both in the masculine family unit of Nicky,

Matty and Errol, and in the interaction between the various officers of different ranks and the local community. In these respects its predecessors include *Juliet Bravo* (1980–85) and *The Bill* (1984–). *55° North* also includes aspects of various other genres, including: romance through the on-off affair between Nicky and Claire Maxwell; elements of the legal drama in the power-suited, snooty barristers of the first series; a strong comedic dimension supplied throughout by sundry uniformed officers forever getting into scrapes; and even some melodramatic moments towards the end of the second series with the prodigal return of Matty's reformed father. *55° North* also imports a US televisual slickness identified by Robin Nelson in shows like *LA Law* (1986–94) and *NYPD Blue* (1993¬2005) as a "combination of apparently fast-action narrative, in a glossy (high production values) style with a range of characters in a 'work family' whose private lives are to the fore" (1997: 184). In *55° North* the action is provided by countless chases on foot through Newcastle at night, combined with narratives involving prostitution, drugs and date rape that showcase the nightlife of the city. Thus the series' generic hybridity reveals its ratings agenda, its high production values adding a glossy sheen increasingly typical in the context of the multi-channel, international television marketplace from which *Our Friends* stood out in 1996. More to the point it uses Newcastle's made over aspect to provide this glossy sheen. Unlike *Our Friends'* social realist approach to life in Newcastle, *55° North* provides a perfect platform for showing off Newcastle's newly gentrified image. The Millennium Bridge makes its first appearance in the first episode of the first series and again at the start of the second (along with the Tuxedo Princess), the BALTIC is featured in the introduction to episode three, and any number of events (from murders to romantic evenings out to court appearances) take place either on the Quayside, or within a few hundred feet of it.

Although following Sparks' (1992: 125) observations it is unusual to see an urban cop show set outside London, in actual fact *55° North* is not so strange. The series exists in relation to a number of contemporaries that represent post-industrial life in various regional cities of England and Scotland, including Glasgow in *River City* (2002–), Middlesborough in *Steel River Blues* (2004), and Manchester in *Life on Mars* (2006–2007). What is distinctive about *55° North*, however, is that its Newcastle setting establishes this "made-over" cop show within a recently "made-over" city environment. As George Brandt (1993) notes, in *Inspector Morse* (1987–2000), "the camera dwells on Oxford with lingering pleasure" offering a "travelogue" (97) view that appeals to international viewers. *55° North* strategically deploys certain areas of Newcastle repeatedly for precisely the same reason. Not only does so much filming take place around the Quayside, the titles also begin with a shot of the Millennium Bridge, and include the Angel of the North, the Quayside and the Tyne Bridge. Nicky's family live in the more scenic end of Tynemouth's seaside community (with its distinctive lighthouse in the background of practically every shot), Claire Maxwell's expensive flat overlooks the Millennium Bridge (which, along with the by then completed Sage Gateshead becomes increasingly prominent in series two), and an unlikely number of crimes take place in the wealthy Jesmond area. In its depiction of the city, then, *55° North* could be considered the televisual equivalent of a film like *Goal!*, attempting to sell Newcastle as an international destination by representing it through its most wealthy vistas.

From Racial Politics to Professional Standards

In *55° North* racial politics are inextricably bound up with the way Newcastle is represented. To understand how the city is depicted therefore necessitates an understanding of the series' racial politics.

The presence of a black cop as a protagonist is still unusual in British television crime drama. As Jim Pines notes, when black officers are featured they are usually engaged in policing crimes within local black communities, their presence as a positive stereotype being outweighed by the continued dominance of negative stereotypes of black criminality (1995: 68). For instance, George Harris, who plays Errol, also starred as the lead in *Wolcott* (1980–81), a previous attempt at focusing a show around a black cop that Pines cites as the clearest example of this tendency. Don Gilet's Nicky, then, often depicted protecting minorities in a predominantly white Newcastle, is obviously intended to counter this tradition under the guidance of his televisual "uncle".

Nicky is also an obvious reaction to several high publicity events that seriously damaged relations between police and Britain's racial minorities in the preceding years. These included: the Macpherson Inquiry into the murder of teenager Stephen Lawrence in 1993, which reported in 1999 that institutional racism existed in Britain's Metropolitan police force (Macpherson, 1999); the BBC documentary *The Secret Policeman* of October 2003 (filmed undercover at a police training centre in Cheshire) which revealed the extent of racism in the force; and continued press coverage of the activities of the British National Party in Britain as it grew in popularity amongst disaffected former industrial communities in the North. Thus *55° North* was obviously intended to address public concerns over racism in the country in general, as well as reports of disproportionately high numbers of random searches of ethnic and racial minorities by the police, and indeed, the difficulties that existed in recruiting such minorities to the force (bbc.co.uk, 2003: "Q&A").

Initially the series directly engages with the almost casual, everyday institutional racism reported by the Macpherson Inquiry. On arrival in Newcastle Nicky is pulled over for, as he puts it, "Driving while black", and Sergeant Rick Astel (Andrew Dunn) deliberately breaks his back brake light in an attempt to provoke him into a violent reaction. Several other such instances occur, including a banana left anonymously on Nicky's desk, and the repeated wry gag of Nicky requesting backup to apprehend suspects only to be mistaken for the suspect by the backup. Most clear in this respect is the third episode of series one, where police apathy towards accusations of racial aggravation made by Ugandan shopkeeper Mr Patel (which only Cole takes seriously), leads to him being badly beaten and hospitalised.

Perhaps unsurprisingly the series' foregrounding of racial issues is always a little skewed towards national preoccupations rather than those more relevant to Newcastle itself. The ethnic and racial minorities that feature in the series include the Ugandan Mr Patel, Nazeer Ahmed, a British born kebab shop owner of unspecified ethnic origin, and Ivan Radic, an illegal Eastern European immigrant worker of indeterminate national origin. These characters, along with Nicky's family, are representative of many of Britain's racial and ethnic minorities. Yet two of Newcastle's most significant minorities, its Chinese and its Jewish communities, are either underrepresented (one harassed elderly Jewish couple appear briefly towards the end of the second series) or completely absent, as is the case with the Chinese community. The image of Newcastle that is created is a microcosm of multi-racial, multi-ethnic England. The appearance of the new Welsh Detective Inspector Bing (Mark Lewis Jones) in series two, locking horns with Irish CPS lawyer Claire Maxwell, and the occasional appearance of various incidental characters from as far afield as Scotland and the Home Counties broadens this image to take in the rest of the Britain, the UK and even Ireland. As I have shown elsewhere, this practice appeared in several British films of the late 1990s, including *Sliding Doors* (1997) and *Notting Hill* (1999), as they re-branded London as a global city in which national identity had supposedly become transnational (Martin-Jones, 2006: 85–120). Although this image of Newcastle as a microcosm of British diversity is perhaps what might be expected of a post-modern hybrid that begins by sending a black policeman called Cole to

Newcastle(!) it also speaks of a larger concern of the series, that of using Newcastle to make a statement about the nation's prosperity.

There are obvious ways in which 55° *North* advances the stereotype of the black policeman, providing through Nicky a much needed positive role model. The most obvious example of these is when Nicky defiantly eats the banana left on his desk, turning a racial slur into a source of energy. This could be seen as a positive reworking of what Pines has previously termed the "deracialisation" (71) of the black cop's identity in the television crime drama. This happens when the racial identity of a black character is subsumed by their identity as a cop. Even so, in the climate in which this series appears its focus on professionalism as a leveller of racial difference could equally be considered as an unrealistic reassurance that, despite the ongoing problems facing the police, black officers continue to thrive. An ambiguity exists throughout over whether Nicky is simply a good black cop, or whether his professionalism deracialises him as "just" a cop able to (or at most, occasionally forced to) shrug of the minor challenges of institutional racism. This ambiguity is clearest in the second series when the racial theme is somewhat sidelined, replaced by that of police corruption.

It actually becomes clear towards the end of series one that many of the events that initially appeared to smack of institutional racism were actually far more benign, if not complementary to Nicky. The most important of these is the revelation that Nicky's boss, Detective Inspector Dennis Carter (Christian Rodska) kept him on the night shift not out of prejudice but because Nicky is the only clean officer he can trust with his suspicions of police corruption. Moreover, after Nicky's initial, apparently racially motivated run in with Sergeant Astel, the two characters soon begin to work more closely together, and it transpires that Astel is not in fact a racist. Astel's character develops into a well-meaning, loyal overweight local cop who has been passed over for promotion in the past. He is a stock type in police dramas, with obvious predecessors like Sergeant Joseph Beck (David Ellison) in *Juliet Bravo.* In fact, when Astel breaks Cole's brake light it is not rendered as a racially motivated action, but that of a man frustrated with his own inability to advance professionally. He does so only after Cole provokes him by citing The Police and Criminal Evidence Act of 1984, suggesting that he was provoked by his own feelings of professional inadequacy. Noticeably – Astel's insult to Cole, "You're a flash bastard with a car like this" – is not racist. This motivation becomes more apparent when Astel approaches Cole for his support in gaining promotion, after Nicky has described him as a "brother officer". The racial connotation of the word "brother" is used in this instance by Cole to point out that race should not stand in the way of their professional relationship.

Moreover, in episode three of series one, when Ugandan shopkeeper Mr Patel is attacked, a clear division is made between Astel and the racist attacker. To draw out the attacker Astel hints at racist feelings, which prompt a racist statement from the suspect. Although Cole comments in passing that Astel's subterfuge was remarkably convincing (suggesting once again the institutional racism of the Macpherson Inquiry), a distinction has been made between real and a performed racism. By midway through series two Astel's unthinking remarks to Cole concerning positive discrimination (that he should have competed for the job of Detective Inspector, as a black man has a better chance than a Welsh man) are used to show that Astel's opinion is best seen as that of a misguided clown – as his dumbfounded colleague's Constable Clark's expression clearly shows – rather than that institutional racism is a continuing problem in the police force. The series ultimately paints Astel as a sympathetic character, particularly through his "Cop Idol" karaoke performance of Bonnie Tyler's *Total Eclipse of the Heart* in series two. Whilst he initially appears to illustrate the casual, everyday and offhand nature of institutional racism, he ultimately renders this problem an occasional "lapse" or mannered, joking performance of a few insensitive but ultimately well-meaning officers.

Several other moments in the series add to this "reassuring" impression that institutional racism is a diminishing issue, including the only occasion when it is actually mentioned. Nicky and Claire Maxwell note how the police are both institutionally racist, and institutionally sexist. Yet this conversation occurs in the context of the show's depiction of Maxwell as an over fussy female lawyer. After DI Bing pats Sergeant Brooks (Emma Cleasby) on the bottom in his office, Maxwell suggests that Brooks file a complaint. Brooks however, who is romantically involved with Bing, tells her to get a life, and later jibes that Maxwell is "frosty". Brooks' position is supported by the series, which uses the humour directed at Maxwell, along with Kirwan's deliberate prissy overacting, to suggest agreement with Brooks' stance. When dealt with in this way, institutional racism appears far more innocuous, as though on a par with a slightly inappropriate gesture between lovers over which too much fuss should not be made. Most conclusively however, in the final instance the police force are redeemed of all charges of institutional racism, when repentant crooked Detective Sergeant Patrick Yates (Darren Morfitt) saves Cole's life, taking his place when he knows it will probably means his own death. If even the most crooked of cops is free of this charge, then surely the whole force is. In the process of rebranding Newcastle the series creates what – following Sparks' 1992 work on the psychology of the televisual crime drama – can perhaps best be described as a reassuring narrative of the diminishing problem of institutional racism in the police (25).

Our Friends begins in 1964 with the return of Nicky Hutchinson to Newcastle after a summer involved with the equal rights movement in the Deep South of the USA. Visiting Mary he finds her family watching *The Black and White Minstrel Show* (1958–78) on television. However, this racial theme is soon transformed into its supposedly equivalent problem in Newcastle, that of class inequality. Nicky's reforming drive is soon channelled towards social housing policy, leading to the controversy over the Willow Lane Flats, whilst the serial itself begins to focus increasingly on governmental and police corruption. This tendency to view the city through the eyes of the returning Geordie has appeared many times before in films like *Get Carter* (1971) and television programmes as diverse as *When the Boat Comes In* (1976–81) and *Auf Wiedersehen Pet* (1983–2004). In *55° North* the visitor to Newcastle is another Nicky, but this time he is an outsider from the start, both regionally and racially. *55° North* similarly uses the gaze of outsider Nicky to explore what the city has to offer the visitor (much as films like *Goal!* do), emphasising the very different approaches of the two programmes. What is interesting about this comparison is that like *Our Friends*, *55° North* also shifts its initial emphasis from racial issues to that of police corruption. However, it reduces this to the actions of a few bad apples rather than reinforcing the condemnation of widespread institutional corruption found in *Our Friends*.

London Lifestyles on Tyneside

To return to Newcastle at this point, it is by shifting its focus from institutional racism towards an exploration of how Nicky has begun to thrive professionally in Newcastle that *55° North* addresses Newcastle's potential as a city.

Most effective in shifting this focus is the equation of Newcastle with London. This demonstrates the way in which the gentrification and subsequent wealth generation that London has enjoyed since the 1980s has now also reached the rebranded North. It also suggests that the North's institutions, including the police, have now been modernized in line with those of London. This conflation of North and South through comparisons between Newcastle with London occurs on many levels. Firstly there is the "Millennium city on the river" graphic match that occurs in series two when Errol and Nicky travel to London to find Matty. Here London is introduced by an establishing shot of the London Eye by the

Thames. This image is the southern equivalent of the Millennium Bridge on the Tyne image of Newcastle. The two architectural Millennium projects on the two rivers suggest the similarity of the two cities. More obviously there is Nicky's success as a fish out of water cop in Newcastle, the ease with which he adapts his skills to this environment again emphasising the similarities between the two cities. This assimilation of the black southern cop into life in Newcastle also implies that existing stereotypes of the parochial, racist North seen at the start of *Our Friends* no longer hold true for rebranded Newcastle. Finally, once Nicky has helped clear up police corruption by the end of the second series the equation of the two cities is complete. Having cleared up the force in London (he was transferred for reporting his crooked boss), Nicky's transfer enables the same process to occur in Newcastle. In *Our Friends* the equation of police corruption in London with that in Newcastle rendered it a nationwide problem. In *55° North* this problem has, apparently, been cured nationwide. Setting the series in Newcastle ensures that the city's physical makeover doubles this institutional makeover. Issues of race, then, are used to enable the series to make its point about the national rebranding of England, a process in which the equation of London with Newcastle is key.

Errol's history lessons for Matty are also extremely instructive in this process. In many respects Errol's tales of his Caribbean childhood in Port of Spain provide a postcolonial acknowledgement of the origins of Britain's various racial populations. As Errol points out to Matty, the blood in his veins makes him more than just English. However, the lessons chosen by Errol actually stress how Matty's Caribbean heritage impacts upon his black English identity. For instance, Errol and Matty's colourful recreation of the carnival in series one unites them with this Caribbean heritage, but also compounds the series' conflation of London (through Errol's tales of the Notting Hill carnival) *and* Newcastle. Matty is being taught about both his Caribbean heritage and his London roots. Similarly, when Matty needs to give a presentation at school on a British hero, Errol teaches him the forgotten history of Sister Mary Seacole, a Jamaican born nurse who became a British national hero during the Crimean War. Errol stresses that this history lesson gives Matty back his identity, but this is a British identity as much as it is a Caribbean heritage, as Errol's story culminates in official British acknowledgement of Seacole's efforts at a regimental benefit dinner in her honour. In contrast to contemporary evidence suggesting that racism is a continuing problem in Britain as a whole, the interaction of Errol and Matty reassures the viewer that, as Errol puts it, "England certainly has changed". Like the movement of the capital's wealth to the North from London, so too have its standards of tolerance also been adopted by the North. Thus, as Fulham fan Matty initially struggles to assimilate himself into the local school, any suggestion of racial barriers to his success are immediately recoded as regional issues. When Errol tells him, "they'll get used to you", he replies, "I don't think so, they hate people from London". In series two Errol even evokes the Bolton based boxing sensation Amir Khan as a role model for Matty, the nationally lauded Northern teenage sensation's press coverage as 2004 Olympic silver medallist further suggesting that intolerance towards minorities is a decreasing problem in England, both North and South.

In *55° North* Newcastle is rebranded as a fully functioning part of post-industrial England. If Geordies are often considered the "cockneys of the North" (Hutchings, 1996: 274), then Newcastle here appears as the London of the North. Most importantly in this respect Newcastle now offers a comparable lifestyle to that found in the global city of London. Not only are there numerous well tailored lawyers with upper class accents enjoying Newcastle's more glamorous restaurants, but even down-to-earth coppers like Nicky can afford a classic car (a Mercedes convertible) and – as is pointedly stressed in one episode – to occasionally wear £100 shirts to work. In the gentrified Quayside area of the Tyne, T. Dan Smith's vision of Newcastle has finally been realised, and the makeover of the Toon that GNER mention in their advertising (from industrial backwater to thriving cultural centre) is now being marketed on national television. As Nelson pointed out in 1997, in the new ratings based environment of multi-channel television any number of shows have deliberately gone out of their way to construct images that reflect the "values and lifestyle" (74) of their target audiences. In *55° North* these lifestyle politics are embodied by Nicky, a thirty something fair cop with a sensitive side and familial responsibilities. His is a healthy, professional body deployed in the pursuit of both suspects and the foxy CPS lawyer Claire Maxwell. It is also an image conscious body, celebrating urban style by wearing £100 shirts and eating in fancy Quayside restaurants. However, it has an upmarket "country" dimension seen in the sanctuary of Nicky's familial seaside residence and his classic car. Thus Nicky's split existence between city and coast ensures that the series appeals to the mass audiences of the South East of England, who can either associate with or aspire to exactly this type of lifestyle. This market orientation further clarifies why North and South are bound up in the series, despite its emergence during public debate over the viability of a regional assembly in the North East.

As I have shown, the televisual image of Newcastle has markedly shifted since the mid-1990s, keeping pace with the rejuvenation of the city. The rebranded image of the Quayside and its nationally recognisable landmarks is deployed in

55° North as part of a larger process of national rebranding which reassures the audience that England as a whole has been made over economically, culturally and institutionally, along with the city.

Bibliography

BARB (Broadcasters' Audience Research Board Ltd). Available at: www.barb.co.uk

bbc.co.uk (2003), 'Inside-Out: T. Dan Smith'. Available at: http://www.bbc.co.uk/insideout/northeast/series2/tdansmith_newcastlepolitics.shtml

bbc.co.uk (2003), 'Q&A: Lawrence Murder Ten Years On'. Available at: http://news.bbc.co.uk/1/hi/uk/2965399.stm

Brandt, G. W. (ed.) (1993) *British Television Drama in the 1980s*. Cambridge: Cambridge University Press.

Cooke, L. (2003) *British Television Drama: A History*. London: British Film Institute.

Eaton, M. (2005) *Our Friends in the North*. London: BFI Classics.

GNER. Available at: http://gner.co.uk/GNER/Destinations/Newcastle-Gateshead.htm

Hutchings, P. (1996) '"When the Going Gets Tough…": Representations of the North East in Film and Television', in T.E. Faulkner (ed.) *Northumbrian Panorama*. London: Octavian Press, pp. 273–290.

Macpherson, W. (1999) Steven Lawrence Inquiry Report. Available at: http://www.archive.official-documents.co.uk/document/cm42/4262/sli-06.htm

Martin-Jones, D. (2006) *Deleuze, Cinema and National Identity: Narrative Time in National Contexts*. Edinburgh: Edinburgh University Press.

Nelson, R. (1997) *TV Drama in Transition: Forms, Values and Cultural Change*. London: Palgrave.

Pines, J. (1995) 'Black Cops and Black Villains in Film and TV Crime Fiction', in D. Kidd-Hewitt & R. Osborne (eds.) *Crime and the Media: The Post-Modern Spectacle*. London: Pluto Press, pp. 67–77.

Sparks, R. (1992) *Television and the Drama of Crime*. Buckingham: Open University Press.

Part Three

Visualising Local Identities

Chapter Nine

Tyneside's Modern Rome:
the North East's Image of its Roman
Past and its Lost Englishness

Paul Barlow

This chapter is about the relationship between historical and modern cultural identities, a subject that is always fraught and constantly renegotiated. What I want to argue here is that the radical de-industrialisation of Tyneside during the last thirty years of the twentieth century has accompanied an equally radical realignment of its relationship with its own past. I will also suggest that this realignment reveals some important characteristics of the cultural management of past and present identities, and of the relationship between the North East and the various historical identities that overlaid one another in the construction of its current incarnations: Celtic; Roman; Anglo-Saxon; Viking; Hanoverian; Industrial; Proletarian and so on.

In the last decades of the twentieth century the transformation of Newcastle itself from industrial to post-industrial city was accompanied with the expansion of a range of visitor attractions dedicated to the display of aspects of its past. This was characteristic of similar developments elsewhere, but was more pronounced in Newcastle because the city had previously had little popular association with the leisure industries, but by the end of the 1990s had become identified as one of the Britain's premier party cities. This transformation was bound up with the slow abandonment of an identity based on the idea of respectable skilled industrial labour, an identity materially incarnate in the pattern of late Victorian working-class housing that stretches with unrelenting density along both sides of the Tyne.

In 2004 the new social confidence of the post-industrial Tyneside was supposed to have been consolidated by a comparable political transformation. A local "yes" vote would have established an elected regional assembly in the area. This idea, strongly promoted by the Deputy Prime Minister John Prescott, was intended to reunify Britain on the model of France, by establishing powerful regional centres that would eliminate some of the inconsistencies created by the devolution of Wales and Scotland. The North East was identified as the likeliest region to support devolution within England, precisely because of its strong local culture. If the North East voted for a regional assembly then there would be no good reason to deny it to the North West, or to the Midlands. Since the devolution of Wales and Scotland in 1998 Britain had been divided between the "Celtic" areas and the "Germanic" (Anglo-Saxon) areas of England. That difference would be subsumed in the now inclusive distinction between powerful but equal regions, in which Scotland and Wales would simply play a part among others. In other words, then, there would no longer be any simple concept of "England" in contrast to Wales and Scotland – there would, instead, be a series of regions, comparable to the French system of Departments. In France the nominally Celtic Brittany is distinct in only the same way as other Departments such as Paris itself or formerly separate nations such as Burgundy.

In fact, Prescott's plan failed utterly. The people of the North East failed to support a regional assembly, apparently because they saw it as no more than another tier of local government, one which would also involve an extra tier of taxation. The vote was an overwhelming 696,519 against to 197,310 in favour. Far from being an act that would liberate local identity it was seen as something that would further *submerge* local culture under a sea of alienating bureaucracy.

This is, I will attempt to show, one of the fundamental paradoxes and problems implicit in North East identity. It is central to both what makes it powerful and what consigns it to institutional inarticulacy. This process, epitomised by the 2004 vote, will, I hope to show, reveal something about the ways in which cultural identities are forged. It tells us why in Scotland an extra tier of government is seen by the majority of the population as a *desirable* development – something that unleashes a long-suppressed sense of national identity. It also allows us to see why, against Prescott's best hopes, an institutionalised regional identity was seen as a *violation* of local culture, an imposition of nannying systems over the free people of a vibrant metropolis.

What I want to suggest here is that these very modern ideas are mirrored by shifting models of very ancient history, and that the decisions made in 2004 were informed by events long lost to most voters in the confusions of the past. But the opposite is also true – that the past is created by the present. Our sense of who we are is strongly determined by how our past makes sense in our present. And this is an equally important aspect of the way in which the past is represented to us.

The North East of England is a uniquely powerful location in which to explore this issue, precisely because its identities have been so varied, so contested and so obscured. It may even with justification be described as an *effaced* borderland between multiple ethnic identities. I use the term "effaced" here because its contradictory and diverse identity is currently submerged by the strong regional persona that has emerged since the industrialisation of the Tyne in the nineteenth century. This distinctive regional personality, going by the name "Geordie", was perhaps originally a reference to the pro-Georgian affiliation of the population of Newcastle at a time when many of the people of the North East were sympathetic to the Jacobites (Colls & Lancaster, 1992: xii). At the time this would have meant that the Geordies were in favour of broadly liberal and progressive politics rather than the more tribal loyalties of the past, an affiliation later confirmed by the inscription on the prominent monument to Earl Grey in the centre of the city. Now the label often implies the opposite: the existence of a distinctive and resilient local identity that resists assimilation to national norms.

This strange inversion of identities is precisely what I wish to explore here, with particular reference to the ways in which modern Newcastle has defined itself in terms of an abandonment of local identification with great industrial heritage of the nineteenth century. It did so, I will suggest, by the increasing equation of the North-East with the legacy of ancient Rome, a legacy which allows for a distinctive negotiation between modern leisure or service based industries and the idealisation of lost heavy industry itself. This articulation of post-industrial identity for the region reveals the ways in which historical cultures are reconfigured in the name of the revitalisation of regionality itself. These historical identities often work in ways that differ meaningfully from the more explicit representations of the changing city in popular culture, as explored in this book by Peter Hutchings and David Martin-Jones. They also work to complicate the relationship to general forms of modernity – in fashion, design and art – examined here by Hilary Fawcett, Cheryl Buckley and Shelagh Wilson.

Imagining Rome on Tyne

The role of ancient Rome in the modern imagination has always been powerful. While the most important aspects of Classical culture have been traced to the ancient Greeks it has always been the imperial Romans who have been the template for later imaginary models of the struggle between Civilisation and Barbarism. While the sacred status of the Greeks went unchallenged, Rome was almost as much vilified as it was praised for its glories. It always came to stand for what modernity needed to see in order to make itself anew. It is Rome that dominates the history of artistic and of cinematic representations of the ancient world, and it is Rome that has worked to signify changing cultural priorities. The Rome of the Renaissance and the Rome of the late twentieth century are very different, but both stand as exaggerated, primary-coloured versions of the world in which the makers of the images lived. This is especially evident in the late twentieth century.

This was also very clearly in evidence in the North East, when the early images of Roman achievement were allied to the claims that the region was growing to create a new identity for itself. William Bell Scott's paintings in Wallington Hall depict the history of the region beginning with the creation of Hadrian's Wall and ending with the urban-industrial modernity of the nineteenth century, towards the painting of which the Roman officer on the wall points, as if the advent of Roman engineering on the Tyne inexorably led to the full majesty of Victorian industrialism. For Scott these two moments in history are intertwined and, ultimately inseparable. One creates the other. As the Roman centurion who oversees the construction of the wall gestures authoritatively to his resentful Celtic workers he points beyond his own known world to the alien and overwhelming modernity opposite him in the space of the room he occupies. Only a few feet away, but representing the struggles and aspirations of millennia, is the scene of industrial production on the Tyne known as *Iron and Coal*, or, more properly, as *The Nineteenth Century*.

The paradoxes implicit in the early North Eastern commentaries on the Romanisation of the Tyne have been explored in detail by Paul Usherwood, who points to the conflict between Scott's desire to present Rome as a modernising force and the liberal traditions that associated it with alien tyranny, antithetical to the modernising processes productive of free peoples (Usherwood, 1996).

Shortly after the huge success of Ridley Scott's epic movie *Gladiator*, a new Roman-themed visitor centre opened near to Scott's own hometown of South Shields. Over the river, at Wallsend, the Roman fort of Segedunum had been chosen to be developed as a major "family" oriented local attraction. Posters advertising the venture depicted young boys dressed up in Roman military costume and advised parents that a visit would be a great day out for their "little soldiers". Wallsend Metro station – a couple of minutes walk from Segedunum – was even decked out with pictures depicting an imaginary Romanised version of the modern town-centre, in which road signs, street names and even familiar shop-names were given in Latin. The local outlet of Woolworths is renamed "Domvs Lana Dignorvm", while the nearby Jobcentre becomes the "Forum Venalicium" (*see Figure 1*). Inside Segedunum itself this conceit continues, as a map is displayed, in the style of the local Metro map, depicting the line of Hadrian's Wall and the roads leading up to it, with the mile-castles listed as though they were stations. The design was "created as part of the PONTIS art project to link the Metro station at Wallsend with Segedunum" (*see Figure 2*).

The imagery creates a fantasy of a kind hitherto confined to alternative-history novels: that the Roman Empire had never fallen. Here we have a mirror of modern

Wallsend, a nondescript suburban shopping centre reinvigorated and re-enchanted – a place that had recovered the status it once had as the final outpost of Western civilisation confronting the wild wildernesses of the north.

Of course the transformation of Wallsend was one of the principal aims of Segedunum. As its name suggests, it had grown up around the end of the Roman wall, its very identity defined by its buried Roman past. Modern Wallsend was a product of the late nineteenth century, when Tyneside's industrial urban landscape expanded rapidly and completely along both sides of the Tyne, swallowing up all the pre-existing villages into a sea of terraced houses and Tyneside flats. The remains of the area's more ancient past were also absorbed into this new, densely urbanised, strip along the riverside, though there was a paradoxical element of disinterment that accompanied the expansion (Divine, 1969: 72). Over the river, directly opposite Wallsend, lay Jarrow, a town with an almost equally ancient past, but one that was also transformed into a hugely concentrated centre of working-class housing. The Anglo-Saxon church and monastery in which the Venerable Bede had written his histories of the early English peoples had become an isolated outpost of pre-modernity in an environment defined by shipbuilding and heavy industry. Elsewhere Roman and Saxon remains were either completely buried or left as unintelligible fragments of an alien world littering industrial suburbia.

The opening of Segedunum, then, represented a kind of *disinterment*, both literal and cultural, of this once-neglected past. During Tyneside's heyday as an industrial centre the Roman and Medieval past was left more or less where it lay, playing little part in the social lives of the local communities of Jarrow and Wallsend. Since the precipitous and almost-complete obliteration of heavy industry in the area, these two locations have been more severely affected than most other parts of Tyneside. Situated in the middle of the urbanised strip along the river, they have not been able to retain the relative prosperity of Newcastle itself and of the coastal regions of Shields and Tynemouth. The rediscovery of lost Roman glory as a form of leisure is closely bound up with the transformation of the area and the emergence of the "weightless economy" of knowledge-based, service and entertainment industries.

Ironically, perhaps, the Segedunum building is adapted from part of the Swan Hunter shipyard, still operational just a few feet away from the visitor centre itself and from the remains of the fort and of the wall's end (*see Figure 3*). On a jutting fragment of fort, Wallsend's late Victorian worthies have inserted a stone commemorating the wall and its builders, whose names appear, inscribed into a plaque on the back. Picked out in now-disappearing red paint, this list of Latin names resembles a war memorial, recording lost engineering glories. This isolated rump of Roman achievement now stands alongside the massive cranes and slipways of Swan Hunter's yard, dwarfed by instruments of modern engineering, as if in vindication of Bell Scott's vision in Wallington Hall (*see Figure 4*).

This is even more of a paradox when set against the emphatically consumer-centred imagery of Romanness at the Metro station, in which the wall-cum-Metro link suggests the facilitation of personal movement across the country. The links are, however, not without their ironies, in particular that very classical-looking Job Centre itself, resplendent with a grand white Doric portico, and rejoicing in the name Hadrian House. The real Job Centre does indeed continue imagery of Roman magnificence, creating a sense that a real Roman modernity might not indeed be so different from the Anglo-Saxon one. A "Forum Venalicium" might still be required, and life may not be so enchanted after all.

Roman Wallsend, then, is replete with paradox, caught in strange transitional position between celebration and melancholic connoisseurship of decay; locked into the assertion of Rome as the fount of industrial engineering and equally as the epitome of a post-industrial economy of retail.

That Tyneside's Roman past has come to epitomise this in recent years is perhaps a product of the fate of the first major example of the modern heritage industry in the area; one which stressed the very weighty traditional industries of the North East. The Beamish Museum was established in 1970 as an open air museum to preserve objects, machinery and other material relating to the history of the area. Its sheer physical "weightiness" is emphasised by its large collection of industrial machinery, and by its reconstructed houses, workshops and railway lines. Beamish was created when the local area was still strongly defined and identified with the mining and shipbuilding industries. It was not simply a memorial to the past, it was repository of memories – defining the process by which the present *came into being*. Since the 1990s this aspect of the Museum has changed its significance, as the communal coherence and industrial progress it celebrates is so much less in evidence.

The Beamish Museum may be said to be related to the concept of *Theatres of Memory*, articulated by Raphael Samuel in his seminal 1994 book on the construction of the modern heritage industry. Samuel's thinking grew out of the traditions of the History Workshop, which sought to recover the details of lived, mostly working-class experience, during the period of industrialisation, as part of a classically Marxist ideology that seeks to promote the formation of a suitable class-consciousness and of independent communal networks in which it can be expressed. In his book this is the aspect of the past that is most fully articulated. He only refers to ancient histories in passing, in particular to early antiquarian historians and to modern re-enacters of the ancient past. It is in this context that a glancing reference is made to the Roman North East, in particular to the:

> ...*ever growing extensions to Hadrian's Wall (a new stretch has recently been opened outside Newcastle) and the building of replicas such as the brand new Roman Gateway at South Shields, which now supports its own legion, the Quintagalorum, a locally recruited re-enactment society which makes a speciality of fourth century drill. (Samuel, 1994: 169)*

Samuel's comments here are unmistakably slightly satirical in tone, playing on the idea that the Roman wall itself is not simply being uncovered but is being artificially extended in some way, and that it is moving away from its natural location in the Northumbrian countryside *towards* the urban centre of Newcastle itself, in which – or rather beyond which – an artificial fort has been constructed, creating a simulacrum of revived Rome. It is not difficult to see the recently faked Latin Wallsend of the Metro station as an extension of this very process – situated between the ever-extending wall and the brand new Roman Gateway in Shields on the coast. In other words, the Roman experience designed for visitors at Segedunum might be defined in opposition to that of Beamish. While Beamish attempts to construct a model of continuity and authenticity – remembered and recovered objects – the new Roman experience is defined in terms of radically reinvented and far more historically alien past.

This tendency to ignore or dismiss the Romanisation of North Eastern popular history is evident in other commentators. Even Usherwood ends his 1996 article with a negative comment on the "Roman forum" in the Gateshead MetroCentre, construing the fantasy of Romanness as a means of "sidestepping the nineteenth century", which was associated with industrialism and squalor (Usherwood, 1996). Similar assumptions are evident in Bill Williamson's 2005 article *Living the Past Differently*, on "historical memories in the North East", which assumes that such memories only legitimately focus on the industrial past, and the marketing of the past transforms "older solidarity" into "nostalgia" (Williamson, 2005: 168). If Williamson retains Samuel's traditional socialist assumptions about history, Stan Beckensall's book *Northumberland: Shadow of the Past*, also published in 2005,

Figure 1: Below: Wallsend Metro Station.

Figure 2: Right: Metro Map of Hadrian's Wall and carved statue of a Roman Soldier, Segedunum.

Figure 3: Bottom: Segedunum visitor centre, seen from the remains of the fort.

Figure 4: Above: Memorial to the builders of the wall, beside Swan Hunter shipyard.

Figure 5: Below: The entrance to Bede's World.

adopts a longer model of historical continuity, centring on communion with the ancient and medieval past. Beckensall's "modern antiquarianism" borrows from nineteenth century Tory emphasis on mystical continuities with Christian and pre-Christian monuments, locked into the landscape. Again, Rome is virtually ignored, a temporary and "alien" presence, almost effaced from the narrative (Beckensall, 2005: 53).

Of course both of these attitudes are built on assumptions about the relation between history and cultural authenticity. Samuel and Williamson view the nineteenth century as "real" history which is being displaced by fakery, while Beckensall seeks a transcendent communion with locality that the ancient engineering works of Rome violated. In fact, Segedunum can reasonably claim to be rather more authentic than Beamish and to meaningfully link ancient and modern engineering in a way that Victorian industrial culture would (and did) understand. It is built over the real site of an excavated Roman fort. Visitors can see the authentic remains of the buildings laid out on the ground. They can also identify the remains of objects uncovered in the nearby museum and can compare these objects with the reconstructed buildings that also form part of the site. Much the same can be said of the South Shields fort (called *Arbeia*: "fort of Arab troops"), in which the excavations continue at the remains, while the reconstructed Gateway and stable-block stand nearby. In these places the reconstructions form part of a continuum of experiences of objects and entertainment, based in the historical authenticity of the remains themselves. They are associated with elaborately family-oriented attractions, particularly evident at Segedunum, which regularly hosts Roman cooking, bathing and other events – accompanied, of course, with the sale of related recipe books and scented bath oils. Here again, community is defined by family and consumption, through which the past merges with the present. The arts initiatives such as Pinsky's map and the locally carved wooden statue of a Roman soldier donated by Scaffold Hill Wood Carving Club in 2000 further promote this process.

In these respects Segedunum encourages a kind of self-conscious *reimagining* of the present, so different from the continuity implied by Beamish. Its interactive displays encourage the visitor to live possible pasts by playing ancient board games and experiencing the effort of holding onto a chain that would lower you into a mine shaft. A mirror above the chain allows you to see yourself in the act.

In part these devices are a development of the somewhat more staid and long-standing visitor centres at Vindolanda and other locations along the wall. The Vindolanda mile-castle has been open to the public under the auspices of the Vindolanda Trust since 1970, containing a traditional museum of antiquities, plus explanatory material, along with the remains of the castle itself (Birley, 1977). This is, needless to say, standard fare at most visitor centres attached to comparable sites of historical interest.

A somewhat closer comparison to the Segedunum experience is the Museum of Antiquities at Newcastle University, which contains the reconstruction of a Mithreaum: an enclosed temple of the god Mithras of the type common in the late Roman Empire. This is presented in its own semi-secret space at the back of the small museum, which is mostly occupied by the usual collection of stelae, jewellery, weapon-fragments, broken statuary, and remains of day-to-day objects. For a small expenditure, the Mithraeum can be activated as a dramatic, almost cinematic presentation in which a Roman soldier explains his religious beliefs to the viewer, while the Mithreaum itself flickers with mysterious and lurid faux candle-light, bathed in a bloody red glow within which can be seen the body of a sacrificed chicken.

In part this event mirrors the unknowability of the Mithraic religion itself, a strange mystery cult, the full content of which was only known to initiates – who never wrote down their knowledge (Ulansy, 1991). The bizarre astrological decorations of the cultic buildings are reconstructed in the Newcastle Mithreaum, along with the totemic costumes, representing various animals, which were used by the initiates in their ceremonies. At the back is a cast of the classic Mithraic altar, representing the god slaying the primal bull. Such imagery functions as part of an attempt to make vivid for modern viewers the presence of a radically alien culture, but the language employed by the actor portraying the Roman officer is thoroughly consistent with the conventions of modern multiculturalism. He invites us to recognise his idiosyncratic activities as a legitimate and equal way of life and belief to our own.

This notion of Rome as both alien and familiar has been a feature of modern encounters with the ancient past ever since the Renaissance, which confronted both the irredeemably alien "paganism" of the empire and its cultural and civic authority as a model for the present. Since then, Rome has persistently been used, openly or implicitly, as a foil for contemporary culture. In the eighteenth century artists such as J.L. David painted scenes from Roman history in a way that mirrored the debates of the day about social values (Lee, 1999: 262–68). David portrayed the disciplined civic virtues on which the Republic was built, in a subject and style that seemed to represent the needs of new revolutionary cultures. Later, when the Revolution collapsed into factional strife, the civil wars of Rome provided a model to represent these modern power struggles. During the reign of Napoleon the glamour of the Imperial phase was co-opted. Later artists used Rome to suggest the corrupting influence of wealth, implicitly connecting Roman decadence to modern cultures of conspicuous consumption and emergent consumerism. This theme was plainly present in early films about Rome, typically connected with imagery of sexual allure and the moral corruptions attending wealth. As in the Biblical *Book of Revelations* Rome became the "new Babylon". Throughout these representations the corruption of Rome was typically tied to its Paganism – Christianity being used as a model of moral virtue through which the empire was both to be judged and potentially redeemed. By the 1950s and 1960s this model was merged with the connotations of fascism and Nazism that Rome could be so easily be used to suggest. At the same time it often came to represent the declining powers of European empires, as its luminaries were typically played by British actors, speaking their lines with classical cut-glass diction. In partial contrast, the twenty-first century Rome of Scott's *Gladiator* was plainly the post cold-war America of George Bush senior's New World Order. Rome, like modern America, was presented as the world's only superpower, portrayed as a corrupted beacon of civilisation surrounded by a sea of bleak and barbaric violence, a culture in which ruthless power politics is mirrored by corrosively lurid forms of popular entertainment used to keep the plebeians happy.

Scott's portrayal of Rome as a mirror image of modern America brings us back to the Rome of Tyneside and the encounter with the Mithraeum, since the film was notable for its complete avoidance of any Christian content or imagery. The central characters are all pagans, whose rituals are centred on the gods of home and family, or of the empire itself. As in the much earlier *Spartacus*, the film portrayed the gladiators as a multi-racial and multi-ethnic group whose class-free camaraderie provides a model of human interaction outside the corruptions of the imperial system itself. This emphasis on the experience of the ordinary individual is repeated at most of these Tyneside attractions. At Arbeia emphasis is placed on artefacts that reveal the interconnections between local people with the Arab-Roman troops, and at Segedunum the information on Romano-British life is intermingled with material relating to work-centred experience during the nation's more recent high-industrial past.

This conflation of different historical moments is perhaps most evident at Bede's World, the principal rival of Segedunum, almost directly opposite it on the south side of the river in Jarrow. Before 2000 this was a small exhibition space in a building close to the church of St Paul and the remains of the Anglo-Saxon monastery in which Bede himself had lived and worked during his scholarly career, in the eighth century. It contained little more than photographs and a few artefacts, along with explanatory material relating to Bede. After a period of closure the building was dramatically reopened in December 2000 as a family-oriented attraction of a type that was mirrored by Segedunum. The rebuilding included the creation of a large new building which mimicked a Roman villa, and through which the visitor was to enter, to be confronted with sententious moral truths in precise roman-font capitals (*see Figure 5*).

The early history of the area was, again, defined by Rome, as the visitor was taken through a dramatic series of rooms providing interactive systems of display which included smells and costumes – in particular monks' gowns in children's sizes. The principal attraction, however, was the farm in which early medieval forms of husbandry were portrayed with live animals of various species and breeds, along with reconstructions of Saxon settlements. Children were encouraged to feed the animals and to participate in other activities.

The Roman-style entrance was designed by the architects Evans and Shalev. Its style was justified on the grounds that it referenced the kinds of building that St Benedict Biscop, the founder of the monastery, would have seen when in Rome. It seems at least as reasonable to assume that the Roman entrance signified a form of secular spectacle of the ancient world that successfully put to one side any intrusive imagery that might be associated too strongly with religion. For this aspect of the visitor centre is one of its most interesting features. Though the bookshop contains literature on the history of the monastery, the display itself thoroughly marginalises Bede's own religious and monastic world. Though there is some discussion of the dispute between "Celtic" and "Roman" forms of Christianity, the centre operates between imagery derived from Rome, which emphasises the mechanics of popular entertainment, and the portrayal of the farm, which reproduces communal life. The actual church itself is kept clearly separate from the visitor centre, which inducts us into its space through the imagery of a villa in a garden – a space representing worldly wealth, power and leisure, if one mediated by imagery of calm, harmony and philosophical contemplation. The experience of the museum conjoins the imagery of leisure and the community.

This then seems to represent the nature of the "Roman" experience as it is articulated in these leisure centres. Rome comes increasingly to represent a kind of consumer-society defined by multiculturalist values but unified by common disciplines. This, I suggest, represents the current self images of the North East more fully than the now slightly-embarrassing lost utopia, represented by the solidarities of mining and shipbuilding industries: communal values sanctified by the museum of Beamish and the writings of Raphael Samuel.

Paradoxes in Imagining North Eastern Ethnicity

This brings us back to that surprising 2004 vote, and its apparent rejection of regional autonomy. It suggests another reason why Rome has come to be the North East's most powerful image of its relation to its past. What that increasingly reconstructed wall always meant was the separation of two realms – the dividing line, as Scott's paintings assert – between modernity and the past; between primitivism and progressiveness. The wall is an emblem of belief in powers of progress that transcend ethnicity.

It has always been the "borderland" quality of the North East that has made it so difficult to construct a mythic continuity of ethnic identity that would stabilise the Geordie persona of the region as a natural outgrowth of ancient tradition. This contrasts powerfully and significantly with Scotland, in which this claim is typically allied to the construction of Celtic identity as a unifying feature. The Celticity of the Scots sets them apart from the Saxons ("Sassanachs") or English. It also confirms the idea that an ancient ethnic barrier has always existed between northern Britain and its central and southern areas. In nationalistic *mythology* "Scotland" was always a separate place – even though in reality the Scots were an invading Irish tribe who did not even arrive until well after the departure of the Romans. The mythic identity of Scotland enables it to appropriate culturally distinctive features into its claims on "Scots" national identity. This is exactly how ancient and modern identities are merged, and powerful myths created. But it can also have the effect that meaning is sucked from other cultures; or at least that another identity is created in order to sustain the mythic continuity and integrity of Scotland itself. The claim that the dialect of "Scots" constitutes a language distinct from the English of England itself has been energetically promoted by Scots nationalists, who either reject pan-Celticism (which of course weakens claims to national distinctiveness) or who feel that the marginality of Celtic languages makes the claim on Scots distinctiveness a far more powerful tool of national pride.

The problem, of course, is that much of the distinctive dialect that makes up "Scots" originated in Northumbria. That fact should not really surprise us, since Northumbria was the focal point of Anglo-Saxon presence in North Central Britain. It was from here that the distinctive form of the English language characteristic of the north emerged and expanded. Northumbria was the beachhead from which the English language spread (Jones, 1995; 1997). It certainly had nothing to do with the Irish Scotti tribes, who intruded into the western coast and expanded from there. The Pictish language, the truly ancient Brythonic (British) version of Celtic speech in the area was assaulted on both sides – by the Irish import from the west, and the Germanic import from the east. Both, of course, were equally immigrant forms of speech, but both rapidly became localised and distinctive to the areas they occupied. North Eastern English spread from its base in Northumberland into the lowlands of what was to become Scotland. The Goeldic (Irish) forms of Celtic obliterated the native Brythonic speech, and soon the two languages were, in effect, competing for control of the nation. Of course it was the expansion of English from Northumbria into the lowlands that proved decisive. This was the area from which modern Scots identity formed itself, even while it fantasised an ancient connection to the old Gaelic clan system of the North.

The result, for Northumbria, is the loss of identity with the ethnic origins of what is – absurdly – termed "Scots". Northumbrian dialect seems as though it is a southern extension of what belongs more properly to the Scottish – something which speaks most fully of *their* identity and distinctiveness.

This loss of continuity applies even to the term English itself, a word which derives from the Angles, a Germanic people who occupied the Northumbria region, and whose dialect was the origin of what became "Scots". The term English is now seen to belong most fully to the south of English. The actual descendants of the Angles are thus less fully English than their Southern compatriots. The Northumbrians are neither fully English nor Scottish, and many of those characteristics that do define them as fully Northumbrian are claimed by other, more powerful, if less plausible mythic identities.

This leads to an important point about the relationship between cultural identity and the dangerous, unstable and myth-violating facts of history. There is, I would suggest, an *absorptive* quality to certain forms of national myth, whereas there is a *dispersive* identity to others. What I want to argue is that the history of Northumbria has become dispersive. This does not mean that its identity has in fact dispersed. The strength of local identity clearly invalidates any such claim. What it does mean is that the historical features – of ethnicity, language, culture – are more effectively appropriated elsewhere. The Geordies are more English than the English and more Scots than the Scots. But they cannot be both.

Here, Rome comes to the rescue. Rome is the defining *origin* of the North East's identity and Rome *in* the North East was characterised by its assertion of a trans-ethnic ideal – of values that negated ethnicity in favour of claims on civilisation and modernity. These were also the very ideals that informed the Hanoverian "Geordie" vision and the model of rational civic progress embodied in the monument to Earl Grey. For many participants in the 2004 debate it was clear that the suggestion that the North should be represented as a separate *region* was felt to be part of the problem. It would "split" England "into bits", as one interviewee put it. Or as another said, "it's kind of like a separation, isn't it, of people?" (BBC, 2004). The Roman wall signifies an inclusion into a modern, sophisticated culture – a decisive rejection of primitive regionality. To reaffirm Rome is also to reject regionalism and to assert that Newcastle is a confidently post-industrial city, a companion to London itself. The New Rome of the Latin Wallsend high street and the visitor attractions of Segedunum and Jarrow builds on the Rome of *Gladiator*, an image of a secularised consumer metropolis of pleasure and prosperity. In this respect the combination of "decadence" and cosmopolitanism that has for so long informed our visions of Rome has come to represent the ambitiously self-disciplined hedonism that is popularly envisaged as the epitome of modern urbanity. Far more than mining, shipbuilding, lost Anglo-Saxon kingdoms or any other aspect of its history that is unique to the North East, the modern city seeks to represent itself as the loyal citizenship of the Roman empire, whose newly renewed wall protects it from descent back into irretrievable provincialism.

Notes

1. The design was created by Michael Pinksy in 2003, and is clearly influenced by Simon Patterson's reworking of the London Underground map entitled *The Great Bear*, in which the station names are replaced by the names of scientists, artists and philosophers.
2. This idea had appeared in same fantasy literature, as well as in *Star Trek*, in which the Romulan Empire represents a high-tech version of Roman culture.

References

BBC Radio 4, Today, 16 June, Regional Assemblies debate, 8.10am.

Beckensall, S. (2005) *Northumberland: Shadows of the Past.* Tempus Publishing.

Birley, R. (1977) *Vindolanda: A Roman Post on Hadrian's Wall.* Thames and Hudson.

Divine, D. (1969) *The North-West Frontier: A Military Study of Hadrian's Wall.* Harvard Common.

Jones, C. (1997) *The Edinburgh History of the Scots Language.* Edinburgh: University of Edinburgh Press.

Jones, C. (1995) *A Language Suppressed: The pronunciation of the Scots language in the 18th century.* Edinburgh: John Donald.

Lee, S. (1999) *David.* Phaidon.

Samuel, R. (1994) *Theatres of Memory.* London: Verso.

Ulansey, D. (1991) *The Origins of the Mithraic Mysteries.* Oxford: Oxford University Press.

Usherwood, P. (1996) *Hadrian's Wall and the new Romans,* in T. Faulkner (ed) *Northumbrian Panorama.*

Williamson, B. (2005) '*Living the Past Differently: Historical Memory in the North East*', in B. Lancaster & R. Colls (eds). *Geordies,* Newcastle upon Tyne: Northumbria University Press.

Chapter Ten

The Newcastle Look:
Culture as Spectacle

Chris Wharton

The Angel of the North, created in 1998, the year after New Labour's election victory, is now a familiar sight, taking its place in a long line of Tyneside public sculptures and monuments. These range from the Roman Tyne god, a personification celebrating place, people and spirit to the nineteenth century figures of Stephenson seated close by Newcastle Central Station, surrounded by industry and technology, and Cowen, on his plinth round the corner on West Gate Road, standing for popular radical politics. As the old millennium faded and the new approached, the Angel was to watch over a renewed air of regional confidence in the North East of England and, many hoped, announce a new approach to regional government, culture and community.

Whilst the 2004 referendum in the North East rejected a regional assembly for the area, two further additions to Newcastle's sculptural pantheon were created in the city centre. Two new metal structures described as "public art" were placed at either end of Northumberland Street, the city's busiest shopping thoroughfare. The semi-abstract figures, were created through stilt-like elongated forms that gave body to a torso emphasised by a circular arm-like movement culminating in a bold, sweeping curve of support to banner bearing poles. Each carried identical abstract emblems of curving yellow arcs on blue backgrounds. Viewed along the vistas of Northumberland Street, the emblems, supported by the 15 metre high structures, mingled with the advertising banners representing the shops and department stores that line this, and other similar shopping streets in many British towns and cities. These standard bearers of consumption symbolised aspects of the city's feel and appearance that, it will be argued in this chapter, announced what amounts to a spectacle of culture (*Figure 1*).

The discussion that follows explores developments in the city of Newcastle upon Tyne that contributed to the promotion of the city through a specific form of cultural identity that relies heavily on image. This promotion has created a discernable "look and feel" to the city: a quotidian visibility, discernible in a variety of forms through a quotidian visuality.[1] The process began in the late 1990s towards the close of a long period of Labour party control of the City Council and continued into the new millennium to create, what the new Liberal Democrat Leader of the Council and others have described recently as a "vibrant...and modern European city".[2] Newcastle City Council, in conjunction with its counterpart in Gateshead, various regeneration partnerships, government agencies and businesses, has been involved in wide ranging urban development. It is reshaping the city through specific building projects such as the Millennium Bridge, BALTIC Art Gallery, Centre for Life, the Sage Gateshead and the redevelopment of the Ouseburn valley. In addition "regeneration" has involved large scale housing demolitions most noticeably on the largely working-class estates of Scotswood and Benwell. In addition to adding numerous new buildings, re-configuring large swathes of the urban spatial layout and making changes to the city skyline, Newcastle has been living through an exercise in marketing and rebranding.[3]

An extensive rebranding of the city has taken place; from the image of a city largely shaped in the industrial revolution and home to the industrial classes and their culture to "a modern business friendly city…with a friendly strong cultural brand image".[4] All this is becoming visually manifest, changing not only how the city looks, but also how it feels, in the way that its residents and visitors experience it. It has resulted in culture as display – a visible spectacle of culture.

As part of this "make over", city public spaces were adorned with banners, flags and drapes hung from lampposts and other city features announcing and advertising aspects of the city, its culture and amenities.[5] This appeared as an extensive marketing exercise rather than a real attempt at street or urban aesthetics (Greenberg, 2000; Moore, 2003). The new-Newcastle brand image appeared along the newly created boulevards that swept traffic into the city; into the bustling shopping areas like Northumberland Street, home to the "standard bearers of consumption", and new development areas like the Ouseburn Valley – but rarely on the working-class housing estates like Scotswood then facing large scale demolition as part of the local authority's regeneration plans.[6] In the city centre, celebrated for its Victorian architecture and recently rebranded as Grainger Town, banners bearing visual and textual statements lined the pavements fronted by the pilasters and columns of traditional nineteenth century, neo-classical buildings. The banners hung outside the concrete and stucco facades of twentieth century modernist buildings and fluttered over the newly paved twenty-first century pedestrianised areas with state-of-the-art, steel and glass street architecture of cycle racks, seating units and waste disposal bins. Slogans, often reminiscent of advertising straplines, decorated the banners with exhortations to "Love the buzz" (the "buzz" was the mythic and spectacular description of the lived experience of the city used by the local authority) or displayed enigmatic single word statements such as "smile", "merry", etc.[7] This created what became known as the "Newcastle look" a post-modern, fragmented civic imagery fluttering above, but far removed from, the social and economic urban realities of the region and the city.

Spectacle over History and Community

The spectacle of culture defined the region's cultural discourse and shaped contemporary outdoor visual culture in the city. The latest project called the "Newcastle Plan and Partnership" is currently shaping strategy on culture and other aspects of the city's future with the aim of "increasing the number of people involved in cultural activities in their neighbourhoods".[8] Critics have pointed to recent evidence that suggests that culture in the city is largely seen as the big statement leading to the big event, where citizen and community involvement is only that of the spectator, the result being that "the city can get lost in its own hype and begin to substitute image for reality, advertising over people" (Chatterton & Hollands, 2001: 136). The big, banal cultural plans, tend to overlook the festivals, concerts, poetry readings, street theatre, and other aspects of the arts and culture that are generated from below. It ignores other more mundane but no less important aspects of culture, the sense of local belonging, the "being-in-community" generated from citizen participation in community activity.[9] The spectacle of culture fails to recognise community-generated culture. The spectacle of culture is merely the latest flimsy layer, as Prospero might have put it, an "insubstantial pageant", hanging limply over the city's substantial frame.[10]

The shape of a city, its look and feel is primarily a development of its history. Pons Aelius, the original fortifications and Roman bridge over the Tyne gave way to the twelfth century Norman stone castle and settlement. This developed into the early medieval layout of Newcastle that involved a spatial shift away from the river and a steep climb up what is now Dean Street and into the industrial period. The development of Grey Street, designed in 1830 by Grainger and Dobson in the neo-classical style, and the streets and buildings that were to become the new centre of the city led to the creation of the theatres, music halls, monuments and galleries that gave shape to much of the urban culture and outdoor visual splendour of the city. The planning and development of the middle- and working-class suburbs, providing homes for Tyneside's industrial workforce, came next. The demolitions of the 1960s, saw the driving of the central motorway through the city and the creation of surrounding high-rise building projects.

Successive bridges crossed the Tyne and symbolised changes in technology and transportation and to the layout of the city: from the first, Roman bridge linking the north and south banks of the Tyne; the successive medieval road bridges; the High Level Bridge taking road transport and the developing steam driven railway; to the magnificent engineering of the twentieth century Tyne Bridge and the less grand, but equally important, metro bridge carrying the electric light railway that helped shape Tyneside as a modern metropolis. Most recently the award winning Millennium Bridge over the Tyne has been a part of the Quayside development and a much talked about aspect of regeneration symbolising Newcastle and Gateshead's togetherness as a joint competitive venture. But the history of the city – essential to its identity – was in danger of being obscured by the recent spectacle of culture.

The spectacle of culture that hangs over the city of Newcastle is a combination of its quotidian visibility and spectacular and manufactured cultural events that demand participation and rely upon the masses for their effect. The new millennium in the city began with a supersized New Year street party accompanied by post-modern street theatre – its themes unconnected to place or history. From here the crowds looked up at numerous firework displays as expensive and striking as they were symbolic of the spectacle. Capital of Culture displays and "love parades" were intended to follow. The Tall Ships race, held in 2005 was marked by a fleet of over one hundred tall-masted sailing ships dropping anchor in the Tyne. The picturesque images of masts set against the architectural splendours of the river's bridges and the crowds milling on both banks of the river were captured in numerous television and newspaper images (Wharton, 2005). Pictures recorded, celebrated, and made newsworthy the event itself and the crowds it drew, and promoted regeneration and development "as seen on" Newcastle quayside. These images featured as "news items" flashed across television screens and printed out on newspaper pages – as similar scenes were formed instantly as personal memories on the screens of the ubiquitous digital camera. Significantly, and symbolically for this discussion of the spectacle of local culture, what was largely absent from the event was any real reference to the reality of the seafaring past (Byrne, 2005). Both the representation of the event and the event itself were disconnected from the history of the river and its locality. All these events were surrounded by and combined with the street imagery of banners, drapes and cultural slogans represented through a hyped-up media publicity machine, in a media soaked promotion of a culture. The spectacle of culture is a product of urban branding an aspect of the "urban imaginary" created through an "ensemble of representations drawn from the architecture and street plans of the city...the images of and discourse on the city as seen, heard or read in movies, television, in magazines and other forms of mass media" (Greenberg, 2000: 228). This spectacle of culture, organised by local authorities and unelected quangos is a response to profound economic, social and cultural change and driven by regeneration and development boards in which private finance or capital is a foremost player.

For the people of the locality, as participants and observers, the spectacle of culture became an increasingly significant element of the lived experience of their city and region. This, in conjunction with other aspects of urban social change, came to challenge older local and community cultural identities often associated with civic citizenship and local political culture based on activities and associations related to place, geographies, histories and traditions. Residual lived cultures were in competition with the spectacle: a competition to represent the city and its people (Jensen, 2005).

The concept of the spectacle was originally developed by Guy Debord in the twentieth century and has recently been characterised as:

> ...the submission of more and more facets of human sociability – areas of everyday life, forms of recreation, patterns of speech, idioms of local solidarity ... to the deadly solicitations (the lifeless bright sameness) of the market. (Boal et al., 2005:19)

The spectacle of culture is about "an unstoppable barrage of ...image-motifs ...aimed at sewing the citizen back (unobtrusively), individually into a deadly simulacrum of community" (Boal et al., 2005: 21). The spectacle of culture requires not only presence and participation at such events as the millennium street parties and Tall Ships race, but a very specific form of involvement: participant observation. The spectacle demands constant observation, representation and replication through the technologies of digital, phone and video cameras. Being there, and looking is not enough. The participant observer captures the spectacle on camera and on video film and at the same time is captured by other participants whilst the media reports and represents the event more widely. What this cultural display is not, or rarely is, is culture based on the unmediated life experience of the people of the region: on their experience of work, life, community and the creativity that might be associated with these things and deemed worthy of celebration.

Quotidian visibility and visuality, the look and feel of Newcastle in the early years of the twenty-first century, is not just as a result of what has here been described as a spectacle of culture, the result of a series of spectacular media-cultural events hyped as part of an ultimate leisure experience. Other contemporary forms and historical factors must feature in an exploration of the most recent manifestation of the Newcastle look. City spaces and social identities have increasingly become associated with consumption rather than production. Although part of wider economic, social and cultural change occurring throughout Europe, economic

Figure 1: Left: Northumberland St, Newcastle.

Figure 2: Below: 2005 Alive.com

Figure 3: Above: Winter Festival 2005.

Figure 4: Left: Welcome Banner, Newcastle.

change and subsequent changes to patterns of work have been experienced intensely in the North East of England. In response to these changes a vigorous promotion of the city and region has taken place not least in selling the place as a "party city". This, in conjunction with Newcastle's bid to win the accolade of City of Culture 2008 and making culture a significant aspect of the local economy, has contributed to the appearance and the everyday visual culture of contemporary Newcastle.

From Work to Consumption

Clearly the city and its local authority were responding to profound economic and cultural changes associated with the decline of the region's industrial economy. In most city centres, productive elements and processes and the social relations of commodity production have disappeared, or tended to move out of the centre and to the periphery of the city territory (Sassen, 1996: 26). This has involved significant changes to patterns of work and wider social shifts. Newcastle's experience was not unlike that of other cities, but the nature of work, based as it was on shipbuilding, iron and coal was less diverse and the effects more widely felt. In a world dominated by image and make over, the industrial past became an unattractive heritage: "to be seen as industrial is to be associated with the old, the polluted, the out of date" (Short quoted in Greenberg, 2005: 6). If the industrial past could not be wholly ignored, it could at least to be confined to the heritage museum business (Howard, 2005). The industrial city, characterised by the making of things; housing, organising and transporting people for this purpose, was now, in its post-industrial phase, to be seen through the prism of its local authority creating policy to address this loss.

Regeneration and rebranding are part of the city's response to post-industrialism and the spectacle of culture was a manifestation of this. Yet, wide ranging cultural change was present even at the outset of the urban working-class's experience of industrialism. The industrial period brought about a loosening of pre-industrial popular cultural forms often associated with a rural, folk culture based on seasonal change, agricultural calendars and religious festivals. A distinctly urban popular culture developed, from the largely commercial such as music hall and cinema to the self-generated community and political events such as the Chartist and trades union rallies, galas, fairs and race meetings associated with the North East. Social groups and cultural activities were represented by many different symbolic banners, themselves the product of distinct but overlapping cultural identities, and functioned as totems of civic, class, political, community and regional identities. The miner's banners still paraded through the streets of Durham each year during the Miner's Gala, and followed by what's left of the local mining communities they represent, are fine examples of the link between the visual, the cultural and identity.[11] Urban culture, some of it still an outdoor culture in the tradition of earlier pre-industrial forms, largely moves indoors assembled around the new mass cultural media technologies of television and radio.[12] The coming of the mobile privatisations from the car to the cell phone, the walkman to the mobile camera seem to introduce a more fragmented culture – one in which a shared communicative space is a less common ground (Chaney, 2002). Other significant features of this culture obsessed with image, include a move towards surface and self-referentiality. Newcastle's Ouseburn Valley, where Tyneside's industrial revolution began – the Coalbrooke Dale of the north, has been earmarked for regeneration. In recent years the area has been adorned with lamppost banners. These stylised representation in blue and green of the nineteenth century road bridge that spans the valley, turn the bridge into a symbol of the area, a rebranding that ironically functions as a signifier of regeneration and change without referring to it directly.

The city's response to fragmented culture was to ferment a new urban culture as image. The re-establishment of a type of urban culture with the crowds forming for New Year's Eve celebrations, spectacular street shows, moving pageants, was encouraged through the promotion of love parades, tall ships races and other spectacular cultural forms. At best this was intended to work against the fragmented aspect of modern mass culture – reassembling crowds as part of a new regenerated outdoor urban culture, communities gathering under the ubiquitous banners, the signs of rebranding. As the banners of regeneration took their place amongst the ever-present commercial advertisements in city spaces this attempt at a new urban culture became visually enmeshed and frequently indistinguishable from the visual signs of a culture of consumption. These cultural changes accompany the economic and social changes that result in cities shifting from identity associated with production to one organised around consumption.

To some extent Newcastle had become, what urban sociologists like to call, an "edge city", a new form of extended metropolis (Garreau, 1992). Byrne has referred to it as "the new urban world without a centre" (2001: 122). Certainly the area undertook a centrifugal transformation, losing most of its heavy industry with little or none of its light industrial production remaining in the inner city area.

What remained moved out to the industrial parks and sites, that fringe areas of the metropolis. But the new urban world of Newcastle was not entirely without a centre; the heart of the city was now given over to various retail, leisure and consumption practices. Newcastle like other cities has claimed new identities and visibilities: "no longer seen as landscapes of production, but as landscapes of consumption" (Zukin, 1998: 82–89). The extension of shopping and drinking hours through deregulation resulted in the city becoming an extensive place, time and icon of consumption.

The centre of the contemporary inner city is now occupied almost exclusively with retailing and consumption, the sales outlets required to market the commodities, attendant practices and transport requirements, spatial requirements such as malls, concourses and pedestrianised ways and the ubiquitous advertisements – from large scale billboards, to adshells and small scale panel ads. Consumption visually dominates the city centre.

Consumption in the inner city can be divided into two categories: shopping for essential commodities often seen as "laborious" consumption perceived as being "akin to work itself" and leisure or "recreational" consumption in bars, cafes, restaurants, clubs and other such places (Prus & Dawson, quoted in Miller, 1995: 106). Leisure consumption in bars and cafes is an important daytime accompaniment to the activity of serious shopping and also forms the core element of the night time city economy.[13] Increasingly, the core city given over to consumption comes to play a significant part in the shaping and reshaping of identities around lifestyle and consumption that are an important element of perceived and lived realities. The visual and behavioural signs of recreational consumption add to the spectacle.

Consumption – and its accompanying activities, discourses and visibilities come to be presented as a form of culture. Behaviour and consciousness; singular, atomised, adrift from the paradigm of production is celebrated in post-modern thought. "(T)he isolated individual juggling with assorted signs and symbols in a never-ending attempt to construct and maintain identity in a fragmented and ever-changing environment", is a potent image of the consumer paradigm (Campbell, 1995: 101). Consumption then becomes associated with culture as identity and consciousness and manifests itself as activity in the looking at signs and purchasing of commodities, taking part in a way of life formed through repeated and significant behaviour through the meanings created for actors and recipients in shared and meaningful spaces. These activities can be viewed as shared cultural activity and a form of identity, increasingly shaped or reshaped through involvement in consumer culture. Urban outdoor advertising and other visual forms such as the city banners are an important visual accompaniment to this. Northumberland Street's standard bearers, the image of which introduced this chapter, stand as totemic and iconic figures around which consumer crowds mingle and the advertising signs cluster, and as "public art", comes to merge with the activity of consumption and culture. A flow of image, activity and consumer identities is formed and takes its place as part of the spectacle of culture.

Consumption as culture features prominently in the presentation of place through local government, commercial and media discourses. For instance, Newcastle City Council chose to identify the city in the visitor's section of its website at the outset of the make over as offering:

> Britain's finest city centre shopping. Its fantastic choice of shops in the heart of the compact city is without equal outside London...national names to elegant arcades, designer stores and street barrows...[14]

Party City and Culture Capital

The local authority has recognised the city's transition from a space of production to space of consumption where consumption features as a foremost element and cultural identity involves both shopping and partying.[15] The party city image was multifaceted, conjuring up the traditional working-class pub drinking culture, but one already changing into a more cosmopolitan "café bar" style or as one of Chatterton and Hollands' interviewees put it "from (a) loutish party image to a more upmarket one" (2001: 122). Making culture an important part of the local and regional economy has involved a shift from culture based on the old industrial working past, to one organised around the idea of "party city" in which visible, commodified leisure is emphatically foregrounded. From Bigg Market to upmarket, the party city brand, as the quote from the city council website indicated, had to be more expansive and inclusive, shifting through class and gender barriers and becoming more associated with culture and the arts. Between 2000 and 2003 the city looked from the Bigg Market to the Baltic for the sense of "carnival and a zest for life"[16] (*Figures 2 and 3*). The council's use of design consultants to design and hang banners in support of the culture bid, from what seemed like every lamppost in the city, was part of this and added to the spectacle. Poorly designed and inappropriate to the task, hundreds of banners adorned the city proclaiming "Newcastle – Gateshead buzzin", "Culture 2008" and flying high in the naff stakes "Love the buzz". The ubiquitous city banners proclaiming the concept of "the buzz" were joined by an extensive advertising campaign that combined this slogan with references to "café bar society" and the city centre's "golden square mile of leisure" creating an image of party city. Who was this aimed at: tourists, potential incoming residents – high banded council tax payers, business investment, employers or was it just an advertising agency's perception to be passed of as the local population's self image and identity?

The everyday look and feel, of recent Newcastle was in part the result of the creation and display of the image of party city in conjunction with the ultra visible forms of conspicuous consumption. A further element – the Newcastle-Gateshead bid to become Capital of Culture 2008, formally inaugurated in the summer of 2001 and led by the Newcastle-Gateshead Initiative – was a necessary third aspect in the creation of the spectacle of culture. An extensive local authority driven publicity and advertising campaign including billboards and other outdoor advertising forms was accompanied by unrelenting saturation coverage in the local media. The knock on effect in the national media was to engage Newcastle in a form of "semiotic warfare" not only with its own industrial past but also with its competitors in the Capital of Culture bid (Gibson, 2005). Despite this, the bid failed. Liverpool won on the basis that it had been more successful in involving the people of the city it represented. Newcastle, on the other hand, appeared to be celebrating a consumption culture rather than fostering cultural production from the communities that make up the city. On the day the winner was announced, Sir Jeremy Isaacs, head of the independent judges, said that Liverpool's stunning dockside developments, its city centre, and strong visual arts, had contributed to its success in gaining the title, more importantly he added, "If one had to say one thing that swung it for Liverpool, it would have to be there was a greater sense there that the whole city is involved in the bid and behind it".[17]

Questions of identity and of cultural identity in a post-industrial city are crucial factors to an understanding of the way that modern urban centres such as Newcastle upon Tyne pursue the question of what it is to be a good city, one that generates a real quality of life for its inhabitants and in so doing creates a modern look that represents the diversity of the ways of life of its inhabitants and contributes to a rich local visual culture of which quotidian visibility and visuality is an important part.

This chapter has charted a recent manifestation of the quotidian look of Newcastle. The look and feel of a city changes and the recent image of the city was always a contested representation. The excesses of the phase of the spectacle of culture based on the party city, conspicuous consumption and the remnant of the failed culture bid appear to be over. Significantly – at the time of writing – the ubiquitous city banners have been much reduced in number, unhooked from many of the lampposts and other structures from which the culture slogans and regeneration advertisements had hung. Those that remain in the summer of 2007 proclaim in large letters a public "welcome" and announce "festivals and events" although details are not included (*Figure 4*). Spaces of consumption continue to grow and swell and efforts will continue to be made to attract investment, employment, tourism and new fangled identities as the city parties on. How the city's visible "look and feel" develops in the future is dependent upon a whole range of policies and factors associated with national and local governance, not least those of city planning, arts and cultural policy.[18] Other less visible aspects of culture, perhaps found amongst forgotten but residual communities or surfacing through emergent cultural activities or organised as conscious cultural activisms, may be working to create spaces and even a politics of cultural resistance to the recent Newcastle spectacle of culture.

Notes

1. Quotidean visuality and visibility refers to the ordinary and familiar everyday images of open public places and spaces and the everyday seeing involved in urban spaces. This latter may involve an element of aesthetic appreciation, but one distinct from a more specific and concentrated viewing associated with art galleries and museums.

2. http://newcastle.gov.uk/

3. Urban branding is an increasingly familiar process and is often accompanied by a redrawing of the environment. The city of Aalborg and the Oresund region of Denmark are good comparisons to make (Jensen, 2005). More generally the phenomenon is well represented by Washington DC in the USA (Gibson, 2005) and by Glasgow in 1990 and more recently by a host of English cities from London to Leeds (*The Independent*, 3 April 2006).

4. Newcastle Plan and Partnership. Newcastle Plan 2004-7. Community Strategy Targets. Available at: http://www.newcastle.gov.uk/newcastleplan.nsf/a/newcastlepartnership. (Accessed: 12 March 2006).

5. Other cities have deployed such devices, in a wide variety of ways, from a celebration of representation of place in Camden, London in 2004 to that of Chineese culture in the 13e arrondisement of Paris in 2006.

6. The original 2002 plan known as Going for Growth anticipated the demolition of 6000 houses and the building of 20,000 new homes to attract the wealthier middle classes to the city. This met with fierce criticism and public opposition against what was perceived as the fragmentation of established communities. These plans were later revised as part of the Newcastle Pathway scheme (see *Newcastle Plan 2004–2007*, Community Strategy Targets). Nevertheless many hundreds of houses have been demolished in Scotswood and further demolition is expected (Robinson, 2004).

7. 'Newcastle is buzzing 24 hours a day.' from Newcastle in the year 2020, Newcastle City Council, City Centre Action Plan 1999/2000.

8. Newcastle Plan and Partnership. Newcastle Plan 2004–2007. Community Strategy Targets.

9. See Jensen (2005) for a general commentary and Byrne and Wharton (2005) specifically on Newcastle.

10. Shakespeare, *The Tempest*, Act IV, Scene I, line 155.

11. Many of the banners carried at the Gala are facsimiles. The originals are often too fragile to transport. See Stephenson and Wray (2005) for a discussion of Northern miners' banners, social networks and community action.

12. Newcastle's Town Moor, an area of open, common ground at the heart of the city, is a good example of outdoor urban space given over to a variety of nineteenth century social and cultural forms. These included semi-commercial race meetings with their stalls and popular entertainments, fairs, and miners' and political reform meetings such as the numerous Northern Political Union and Chartist gatherings.

13. As Chatterton and Hollands have noted, Newcastle's night time, leisure economy of bars, clubs and too a lesser extent restaurants that provide 'nights out in the contemporary period (are) at least partly explained by a search for community and identity in the changing post-industrial city' (2001:76). The authors are referring to the participants in the nighttime economy – those 'gannin oot on the toon' – but this could also serve as an account for the city's search for identity in its adoption of the 'party city' label as a response to social and economic change.

14. http://www.newcastle.gov.uk/

15. 'Newcastle – a great city – once in the forefront of 19th century industrial innovation, now, the

forefront of technical innovation, leisure and culture. Newcastle is rapidly becoming one of the top UK destinations for short breaks, not just the "Party City", but a city that welcomes everyone – passionate, resilient, inventive, with a sense of carnival and zest for life.' Available at: http://www.newcastle.gov.uk/

16. Newcastle-Gateshead Initiative press release, 2001.

17. *The Guardian*, 5 June 2003.

18. The Newcastle-Gateshead Initiative, the team responsible for putting together the bid for the European Capital of Culture, has devised a further strategy, culture10. A study by PricewaterhouseCoopers predicted that culture10 will double the investment in culture, the number of jobs created through culture and tourism and the number of people taking part in cultural programmes. It will, they say, create '24,000 new jobs and £1.2bn investment in the region'.

Bibliography

Boal, I., Clark, T. J., Matthews, J. & Watts, M. (2006) *Afflicted Powers: Capital and Spectacle in a New Age of War*. London: Verso.

Barnard, A. (2004) 'The legacy of the Situationist International', in *Capital & Class*, no. 84, Winter, pp. 103–124.

Byrne, D. (2001) *Understanding the Urban*. Basingstoke: Palgrave.

Byrne, D. (2005) 'Tall ships – the reality of the Tyne', in W. Lancaster (ed.) *Northern Review*, Vol. 15, pp. 67–71. Newcastle upon Tyne: Northumbria University Press.

Byrne, D. & Wharton, C. (2004) 'Loft Living', in *Capital & Class*, No. 84, Winter, pp. 191–197.

Campbell, C. (1995) 'The Sociology of Consumption', in D. Miller (ed.) *Acknowledging Consumption*. Routledge: London.

Chatterton, P. & Hollands, R. (2001) *Changing Our 'Toon': Youth, nightlife and urban change in Newcastle*. University of Newcastle: Newcastle upon Tyne.

Chaney, D. (2002) *Cultural Change and Everyday Life*. Basingstoke: Palgrave.

Garreau, J. (1992) *Edge City*. New York: Doubleday.

Greenberg, M. (2000) 'Branding Cities. A Social History of the Urban Lifestyle Magazine', in *Urban Affairs Review*, 36 (2), November 2002, pp. 228–263.

Howard, S. (2005) 'History, Heritage and Region: The Making of Beamish and Bowes, A Question of Class', in *North East History*, 36, pp. 90–112.

Jessop, B. (1997) The Entrepreneurial City. Re-imagining localities, redesigning economic governance, or restructuring capital?, in N. Jewson & S. Macgregor (eds.) *Transforming Cities: Contested Governance and new Spatial Divisions*. London: Routledge, pp. 28–41.

Jensen, O. (2005) *Branding the Contemporary City – rebranding as Regional Growth Agenda.* Plenary Paper: Regional Studies Association Conference. Regional Growth Agendas. Aslborg, May.

Miller, D. (1995) *Acknowledging Consumption.* Routledge: London.

Moore, E. (2003) 'Branding Spaces: The Scope of New Marketing', in *Journal of Consumer Culture,* 3(1), pp. 39–60.

Sassen, S. (1996) 'Rebuilding the Global City', in A. King (ed.) *Re-presenting the City.* Basingstoke: Macmillan.

Sassen, S. (2005) 'The repositioning of citizenship and alienage: Emergent subjects and spaces for politics', in *Globalizations,* 2 (1), pp. 79–94.

Smith, K. (1999) 'From Ships to Shops', in A. Flowers & Histon, V. (eds.) *Water under the Bridges.* Newcastle upon Tyne: Tyne Bridge Publishing.

Stephenson, C. & Wray, D. (2005) 'Emotional regeneration through community action in post-industrial mining communities: The New Herington Miners' Banner Partnership', in *Capital & Class,* 87, Autumn, pp. 175–199.

Wharton, C. (2005) 'Tall ships: taller stories' in W. Lancaster (ed.) *Northern Review,* 15, pp. 63–66. Newcastle upon Tyne: Northumbria University Press.

Zukin, S. (1998) 'Urban Lifestyles: Diversity and Standardization', in *Space of Consumption in Urban Studies,* 35 (5/6), pp. 825–39.

Chapter Eleven

Tyneside's "Artistic Renaissance" and Art

Paul Usherwood

"All you need for an artistic renaissance is an angel" announced an article on the cultural delights of Tyneside in a national paper in April 2006 (Tom Williams, 2006).

> *The mines had closed, shipbuilding had left and, for an area where pride itself was the core of identity, it seemed there was nothing to be proud of. Then came the Angel of the North. The benefits were massive. Artistic investment brought other sorts of investment; culture became the economic lubricant that greased the wheels of urban regeneration. By 2005, the banks of the Tyne were home to a museum of modern art, a world-class music centre and a millennium bridge so simple and elegant that it made London's look like a cut-price imitation. The Angel and all that came after awoke a passion for the arts that is impossible to ignore.*

Two months later, an audience of arts administrators from around the world at the World Summit in Arts and Culture at the Sage Gateshead heard more or less the same story from Lord Puttnam. Back in the 1980s, the one-time film producer and nowadays cultural panjandrum told them, Gateshead decided to put its faith in visual art. Unfortunately, however, there was a problem; it did not have any galleries. (Like others before him, he appeared to forget that Gateshead does in fact possess a public art gallery, the Shipley, and has done so since 1917.[1]) It therefore decided to put all its efforts into public art. And this attracted approving comments: so much so that it felt emboldened to stage "Festival Landmarks" as part of the Gateshead National Garden Festival in 1990, a huge exhibition of temporarily sited works, said to have been the largest such exhibition ever held in Britain. This then in turn led to the Angel, erected in 1998, and out of that came, as Puttnam assumed his audience would know (which indeed, it seemed, most of them did), Tyneside's current resurgence as an area.

This is a bit economical with the facts but not wholly inaccurate. Since it was erected, indeed even before, Gormley's £800,000 winged colossus has proved remarkably effective as a marketing device. Single-handedly, or whatever the appropriate term is in its case, it has created a buzz. This, however, has less to do with its merits as a piece of sculpture than the fact that, whenever and however images of it are reproduced, it is always instantly recognisable (Usherwood, 2001). It therefore works as a brand image in much the same way as the McDonalds Golden Arches or the Nike swoosh. In fact it works so well that even now, eight years after the sculpture itself actually appeared, picture editors regularly turn to it whenever they have a story about the North, regionalism or, sometimes it seems, anything else to illustrate.[2] And nowhere are the benefits of this media friendliness more apparent than in the town that commissioned it: Gateshead. Whereas back in the 1930s, Gateshead was famously described by the writer J.B. Priestley as devoid of "urban civilisation" – somewhere that seemed to have been "planned by an enemy of the human race in one of its more exuberant aspects" (Priestley, 1934), in 2002 it was listed by *Newsweek* as one of the top eight cultural centres in the world. This might seem absurd. However, it is worth noting, a year after that, Newcastle and Gateshead, now for marketing purposes merged together as one city, came very close to being voted Britain's European City of Culture.[3] No wonder then that a number of towns and cities around the country, for example North Shields, Darlington and Manchester, have resorted to commissioning a landmark artwork of their own in the last few years.[4]

Yet while there is no questioning the Angel's PR success, the social and economic benefits it has brought seem less clear-cut. Certainly a new culture-leisure zone has sprung up on the Newcastle and Gateshead Quaysides, an area where before there were only broken-down sheds and crumbling Victorian offices. And certainly business confidence on Tyneside has generally improved. However, on the debit side, there is something somewhat soul-less about the new Quayside. While the number of people living there has greatly increased, at street level the area often seems empty and lacking in life; only very recently, for example, has a food shop (a Tesco Express inevitably) appeared. As with other such developments elsewhere, for instance Bilbao (see Bradley, 1997), it is a place that seems to be catering almost entirely for those with money and/or a liking for art and music. And the new jobs, that have come along in bars, hotels, restaurants and cultural amenities in the area – nearly a hundred, it is said, in the galleries and restaurants of the Baltic alone – have for the most part been poorly paid, short-term and lacking in security, the kind of jobs in fact that customarily only students and aspiring artists are willing to take.

Needless to say, the cheerleaders for regeneration talk of a "trickle down effect" (Bailey, 2006: 47). A recent Arts Council document, for instance, claims that the Baltic Centre for Contemporary Art and the Sage Gatshead between them have been the catalyst for a £1 billion scheme for the redevelopment of East Gateshead which will eventually lead to the creation of 10,000 new jobs (Arts Council of England, 2006: 36). This of course, will be wonderful if it happens. In the meantime, however, it is still the case that if you venture beyond the confines of the quite small area that constitutes the Newcastle and Gateshead Quaysides, you quickly find yourself somewhere that seems pretty deprived. And indeed this impression is confirmed by government figures which show that the North East has the highest rate of unemployment in the UK and the lowest GDP in mainland

Britain. Indeed, you might be forgiven for thinking that after a decade and more of arts-led regeneration all that has really changed is that the North East's perennial difficulties have to some extent been masked (*Figure 1*).

Yet while it is clearly important to find out about the economic and social consequences of Tyneside's regeneration efforts, that is not what I am principally concerned with here. I am concerned more with something which tends to receive hardly any attention, namely the nature of the art underpinning the regeneration. And my sense is that on the whole (there are exceptions which I will come to) this has been disappointing. Although what has appeared has proved popular (a recent survey shows that a greater proportion of the local population visits arts venues than is the case in any other comparable area of Britain) it has signally failed to meet what many critics believe to be the key challenge for adventurous, significant art in our time which is to provide some kind of site of resistance to the logic, values and power of the market.[5] And the reason why this is so is that it is itself a product of the market; it has come about not for its own sake but for largely instrumental reasons: to further an essentially economic agenda.

What is called public art illustrates what I mean. Local authorities on Tyneside are proud that the area has seen an extraordinary proliferation of permanently sited artworks in the last decade. In fact, Tyneside now has the greatest concentration of recent public art in Britain (Usherwood, 2000: 20). However, when one looks more closely it is clear that the main reason is simply that a developer, planner or owner has decided that a piece of public art would a good way of disguising, enhancing or in some way redeeming some undistinguished new building or piece of urban planning. Naturally there is much talk of how appropriate to their setting certain newly erected pieces are. However, for the most part that is all it is – talk. For in almost every instance it is clear that such pieces would mean more or less the same wherever they were installed, as is confirmed by the fact that some of them have indeed been erected earlier elsewhere. Colin Rose's *Rolling Moon* (1990), (*figure 2*) for example, which now seems to spring up above the trees on the Gateshead riverside a little to the west of the Quayside was originally installed at the Garden Festival in Glasgow. And Sean Henry's *Man with Potential Selves* (2003), now in lower Grainger Street in the centre of Newcastle, first appeared in a sylvan glade at Goodwood Sculpture Park in West Sussex.

Give and Take, a 40 tonne glacial boulder carved by the West Country sculptor Peter Randall-Page, epitomises what I find dispiriting about so many of the new

*Figure 1: Above: Baltic, Sage
Gateshead and Millenium
Bridge.*

Figure 2: Left: Colin Rose,
Rolling Moon, *1990.*

Figure 3: Above: Peter Randall-Page,
Give and Take, 2005.

Figure 4: Workplace, Gateshead.

works that have appeared (*Figure 3*). It was installed in 2005 in front of a new office development called Trinity Gardens behind the Law Courts on the Newcastle Quayside where, according to a leaflet issued by Newcastle Council, it serves to remind passers-by that in former times a stream, the Pandon Burn, ran down to the Tyne past the spot. (Presumably, they are meant to think of it as a stone that has been washed downstream by the current.) This on the face of it might sound fine. However, I would argue the truth of the matter is that, even if passers-by are aware that this is what it is saying (which I very much doubt) it is not actually very helpful for it does not really help them find out how and why the place as it is now.

Something similar might be said about the Angel. The reason why the Angel was commissioned was clearly not that Gateshead councillors suddenly felt a need for an art work which would prompt people to think politically as citizens rather than as tourists either about Eighton Banks, the part of Gateshead where the sculpture now stands, or about Gateshead and Tyneside generally. Nor was it that they suddenly developed an enthusiasm for the artist's work and accordingly felt the need for something by him on their patch. Indeed, I remember meetings in Gateshead before the sculpture appeared at which it was very clear that the councillors present were not in the slightest bit interested in either Gormley's art or his thoughts about what the Angel would mean All they were really interested in was whether or not the proposed sculpture would have the same effect on their town as the Statue of Liberty and the Eiffel Tower had on, respectively, New York and Paris, that is, whether or not it would grab the world's attention and thus give it the kind of competitive edge in city marketing terms it craved.[6]

The thinking behind most public art on Tyneside is in fact thoroughly instrumentalised and this is also true of gallery art, for instance the kind of gallery art found at the Baltic Centre for Contemporary Art, the world's largest temporary exhibition space dedicated to contemporary art. Now I realise it is rash to make definite pronouncements about the Baltic for it is still very new (it opened in July 2002) and it has already had three different directors. Indeed, the present director, Peter Doroshenko, has recently signalled in a public lecture that he and his newly-appointed Head of Programmes, Jérôme Sans, may well be pursuing a very different programming policy in the near future.[7] Nevertheless, I think it is clear that the key criterion as regards the art on show will continue to be not so much its intrinsic worth in purely artistic terms as whether or not it suggests that the Baltic is internationally significant – "world class" in regeneration jargon – and therefore by implication likely to sustain NewcastleGateshead's claim to be a coming area worth visiting and investing in.

Take the line-up of exhibitions in May 2006. It was not untypical. It comprised an exhibition of Sam Taylor-Wood's videos and photographic works, an installation by the Chinese artist Wang Du in the form of a walk-in tunnel decorated with screens showing TV images from around the world, and abstract paintings by two lesser known artists, James Hugonin and Ian Stephenson, one of whom has, and the other had, personal connections with the North East: in other words, on the face of it, a nice, varied mix of video and installation and conventional easel painting, international work and work by "local" artists. However, I would argue that it was actually little different from the kind of mix you might come across in almost any art museum or kunsthalle specialising in so-say avant-garde "elite" art anywhere in the world. That is to say, it was art that had precious little critical edge about it. And this was true even of the Wang Du for in the way that this particular work was installed it registered as little more than an entertaining, fairground-like addition to the spectacle of TV, the very phenomenon which presumably it was meant to be seen as attacking. Nor, it should be added, did the Baltic in its wall texts and leaflets make any great efforts to persuade visitors otherwise.[8] On the contrary, the main point it seemed at pains to convey about both Wang Du and the other exhibitors was that they were big names on the world stage.

But then why would it? The former flour mill cost £46 million (mainly of Lottery money) to turn into an art gallery and is likely to cost further millions (mainly of Lottery money) to run. The director and his team are therefore hardly likely to see themselves as, to quote the critic Benjamin Buchloh, in the business of subversion, resistance, critique and visions of utopian aspiration (Foster, 2004: 673).[9] Or at least not mainly. Besides, they realise full well that people go to the Baltic on the whole not so much for the exhibits as such as for the shop, the various bars and restaurants and the Viewing Box on the fifth and sixth floors with its extraordinary view of bridges and buildings of every age stacked up on the other side of the river. If people want subversion, resistance, critique and visions of utopian aspiration they can look for such things in one or other of the various small artist-run galleries that have sprung up in various down-at-heel, un-touristy parts of Tyneside.

Or so you might assume. In fact, they are unlikely to find them there either. For even in the case of the two most lively and interesting of these small, publicly-subsidized, so-called "alternative" galleries, Vane on Forth Banks in Newcastle and Workplace (*Figure 4*) at the foot of the multi-storey car park in Gateshead, the artists in charge are clearly willing participants in the international art system, a system which, as anyone who flips through the advertisements in, say, *Frieze* or *Artforum* will appreciate, is becoming ever more commercial and homogeneous in character. That is to say, their aim is to try to emulate successful private galleries in the big metropolitan centres by showing work from outside the region as well as inside, taking shows abroad to art fairs in places such as New York and Miami and ensuring that the artists they represent are reviewed in the kind of art magazines that are noticed internationally (Arts Council of England, 2006).

Perhaps it is fitting therefore that the most obvious manifestation of Tyneside's "artistic renaissance" is the dramatic, £70 million Norman Foster-designed Sage Gateshead Music Centre that dominates the Gateshead waterfront. For in some ways the Sage perfectly embodies the kind of instrumentalized, or, more accurately, self-instrumentalized, art that I am saying Tyneside's much-vaunted arts-led urban regeneration has depended on and in turn promoted. It does so in two ways. First, it brandishes a name which has no connection with music but is that of a locally based software company that had the commercial nous to realise that for a mere £6 million it could ensure its name would appear for evermore wherever and whenever the music centre and its activities are mentioned.[10] And second, it is housed in a building that functions, and no doubt was designed to function, as a simple and dramatic visual symbol of Tyneside. Look at the wavy lines of the exterior shell and see how these manage to make the new concert hall seem at once rooted in the locality (by echoing the arch of the nearby 1928 Tyne road bridge) and internationally significant (by alluding to all the other deliberately iconic structures that Foster famously has created for cities around the world).

However, if this picture of the contemporary art scene on Tyneside that I am painting seems too depressing let me end on an upbeat note by mentioning two art organisations which, it seems to me, suggest that something rather different and altogether more hopeful may quietly be going on as well. The first is Locus +, the nowadays four-person commissioning agency that I have mentioned already, which in its present guise, and before that as, first, the Basement Group, and then Projects UK, has built up a formidable and deserved reputation for the way it enables artists to make work that does not simply function instrumentally but is valuable in and of itself (Grayson, 2007). A good example of the kind of project it has been responsible for is Graham Gussin's *Illumination Rig* which appeared for a few cold nights in December 2006. This consisted of a number of very powerful floodlights which illuminated, as if for a night-time scene in a film, a scruffy, left-over, little-visited area of wasteland between walkways and buildings behind Dean St, off the Newcastle Quayside. Now admittedly, in as much as it was commissioned as part of "Glow", the visual art component of the 2006 "NewcastleGateshead Winter Festival", this could be seen as just another exercise in culture-led city boosterism. However, in practice I do not think it was. For it was unlike other pieces in "Glow" and unlike the kind of public artworks that have appeared on Tyneside in recent years as much as it did not serve to decorate the space it was in or add a note of whimsy; it raised questions – questions about how and why "forgotten" pockets of land like this are as they are and how we as passers-by go about endowing them with meaning.

The other organisation I would like to mention as offering hope for the future is Star and Shadow, an 80-seat cinema and performance space with studios and bar attached that a group of young filmmakers, visual artists and musicians in the region, with the help of friends from around Britain and abroad, are currently in the process of building – building with their own hands – inside the former Tyne Tees warehouse at the top of Stepney Bank.[11] What particularly makes this different is not so much the kind of material it shows – artists' films, politically engaged films, gay and lesbian films and the kind of foreign and classic films that in the past would have been shown late at night on BBC2. It is the fact that the individuals and groups who organise its programmes and events do not see themselves as answerable in the normal way to the actual or supposed needs of funders. For sure, they occasionally accept money from bodies like the Arts Council, Newcastle City Council or Northern Film and Media. However, when they do the amounts concerned tend to be small and come in one-off payments. Unlike organisations like the Baltic and Sage ticket sales, donations and the proceeds of bar are what, on the whole, they depend on.

Star and Shadow is therefore, it seems to me, similar to Food, the legendary restaurant that the artist Gordon Matta-Clark and his then-partner ran in a down-at-heel corner of Lower Manhattan in the early 1970s as a haven for the likes of Robert Rauschenberg and Don Judd to eat and party, have productive conversations, make art and show art and sometimes help out in the kitchen (Lee, 2001: 68–72). Which is ironic for it means that in a way it perhaps warrants the label "art factory" which Sune Nordgren, the Baltic's first director, liked to use of the Baltic in its early days. In the event, the Baltic never seemed like a factory, that is, a place of production as well as of consumption. But that is not true of Star and

Shadow. Furthermore, Star and Shadow is not, and never will be, part of the globalised and marketised international art system. This is because, first, it is not under any obligation to attract large audiences, due to the fact that it is located on the edge of the Ouseburn, a part of Newcastle which although fast becoming gentrified is unlikely in the foreseeable future to be subject to the kind of real estate pressures that would kill off such a venture were it to be attempted, say, on the Quayside. The reason it has come about is because some owner, developer or planner has decided that a new arts amenity was what was needed – would nicely augment the "portfolio" of attractions that the area can boast. It is simply because a number of filmmakers, artists, activists and enthusiasts felt that such an organisation was what was needed for them to pursue their own artistic and political interests.

Notes

1. Somebody who also made this claim was Cllr Sid Henderson at a public meeting in Gateshead Council Chamber in early 1995 called to whip up support for the erection of Antony Gormley's Angel at a time when it was still often being attacked locally. See Paul Usherwood (1995) 'A Wing and a Prayer', *Art Monthly*, March.

2. For example, two things the Angel has been used to advertise are BBC 1 (it was one of the famous British landmarks past which a balloon decorated with a map of the world floated) and New Labour (the brochure for the London Fabian conference, Winter 1998).

3. The two towns were first linked together in this way in 2002: see Newcastle and Gateshead Councils (2002) *Building Bridges: a strategy for culture, NewcastleGateshead 2002-2009*, Newcastle and Gateshead.

4. I am referring to Mark di Suvero's *Tyne Anew* (2000) North Shields, David Mach's *Train* (1997), Darlington, and Thomas Heatherwick's *B of the bang* (2001), East Manchester.

5. A study of fourteen British cities conducted for the TV channel Artsworld (*The Guardian*, 30 December 2006) put Newcastle in first place in terms of the proportion of the local population visiting local arts venues. London, interestingly, came ninth.

6. See the leader in the *Newcastle Journal*, 4 February, 1995, entitled 'We'll have an Eiffel' and also an article on Cllr Sid Henderson, Chair of the Gateshead Council, entitled 'Wor Sid's on the Side of the Angels', *Newcastle Journal*, 2 September 1994). 'What I'm interested in is improving Gateshead's image internationally', Henderson is quoted as saying.

7. Northumbria University, 28 November 2006.

8. The one exception to this was a TV screen tucked away in a side room which showed a video of James Hugonin in his garden talking about how the peculiar quality of light in north Northumberland affects his work.

9. See Benjamin Buchloh's contribution to the roundtable discussion on the predicament of contemporary art in Foster *et al.* (2004) *Art Since 1900: modernism, antimodernism, postmodernism*, London: Thames and Hudson: p. 673.

10. I am drawing here on the contribution of Lucy Bird, the Sage's marketing officer to 'A Model Public Private Sector Partnership' at 'The World Summit on Arts and Culture', The Sage Gateshead Music Centre, Gateshead, June 2006.

11. In an interview on 14 October 2006, Christo Waller, one of Star and Shadow's leading lights, cited various ventures in Britain, Belgium and Germany as models, especially The Cube in Bristol.

Bibliography

Arts Council of England (2006) *Turning Point: Arts Council of England, A Strategy for the Contemporary Visual Arts in England.*

Bailey, C. *et al.* (2004), 'Culture-led Regeneration and the revitalization of identities in Newcastle, Gateshead and North-East England', *International Journal of Cultural Policy*, 10 (1).

Bradley, K. (1997) 'The Deal of a Century', *Art in America*, July.

Foster, H. *et al.* (2004) *Art Since 1900: modernism, antimodernism, postmodernism.* London: Thames & Hudson.

Grayson, R. (2007), This will not happen without you: From the collective archive of The Basement Group, Projects UK and Locus + (1977-2007). Sunderland: University of Sunderland Press.

Lee, P. (2001) *Object to be destroyed: the work of Gordon Matta-Clark.* Cambridge, Mass: MIT Press.

Martin, S. & Thompson, E. (2002) *Baltic: the Art Factory.* Gateshead: Baltic.

Priestley, J.B. (1934) *English Journey.* London: William Henmann & Victor Gollancz, p. 301.

Usherwood, P. (1997) 'A Wing and a Prayer', *Art Monthly.*

Usherwood, P. *et al.* (2000) *Public Sculpture of North East England.* Liverpool: Liverpool University Press.

Usherwood, P. (2001) 'The Media Success of Antony Gormley's "Angel of the North", *Visual Culture in Britain*, 2 (1), March, pp. 35-46.

Williams, T. (2006) 'All you need for an artistic renaissance is an angel', *Observer*, Review section, 9 April.

Contributor Biographies

Paul Barlow is Lecturer in Art History at Northumbria University. He has written on the work of the Pre-Raphaelites and other aspects of Victorian culture.

Peter Beacock is Director of Architecture and of the Architecture Group within the School of the Built Environment at Northumbria University. He is involved in teaching, research and practice.

Cheryl Buckley is a Professor of Design History at Northumbria University, and Associate Dean for Research and Consultancy in the School of Arts and Social Science. She researches everyday life, writing on subjects including ceramics, fashion and housing.

Thomas Faulkner was Senior Lecturer in the History of Architecture and Design at Northumbria University from 1974–2004. He has published widely, especially on North Eastern topics and is currently Visiting Fellow in the School of Historical Studies at Newcastle University.

Hilary Fawcett is Senior Lecturer in Media and Communication at Northumbria University. Her research interests include fashion and gender in Britain in the nineteenth and twentieth centuries and regional cultural identities.

Tobias Hochscherf is Lecturer in Film and Television Studies at Northumbria University. His research interests include exile and diasporic film making, films and televisual representations of the Cold War period, contemporary German television and cinema.

Peter Hutchings is Reader in Film Studies at Northumbria University. He has published extensively on British Cinema and popular film genres.

Paul Jones is Programme Leader for Architecture in the School of the Built Environment at Northumbria University. He contributes to teaching of design, and Architectural History and Theory. He has researched and published on regional Architectural History.

Sarah Leahy is Lecturer in French and Film at Newcastle University. Her research interests include stardom, cinema audiences and theories of spectatorship in French Film History.

James Leggott is Lecturer in Film and Television Studies at Northumbria University. His research interests include contemporary British film cultures, traditions of Realist Cinema and the work of the Amber Film Collective.

David Martin-Jones is Lecturer in Film Studies at St Andrews University. He has published widely and his research interests focus on questions of national identity in a range of cinemas from around the world.

Chris Wharton is Senior Lecturer in Media and Communication at Northumbria University and Programme Leader for the Degree in Advertising. His research interests are in culture and political development.

Shelagh Wilson is Senior Lecturer in Design History at Northumbria University. She has published on Victorian and contemporary design.

Paul Usherwood is Senior Lecturer in Art History at Northumbria University. He has published widely in the field of nineteenth and twentieth century Art History and writes frequently on contemporary art, notably in *Art Monthly*.